ULTIMATE BASS FISHING LIBRARY

TOP TECHNIQUES OF THE BASS PROS

MONTGOMERY, ALABAMA

INTRODUCTION

FISHING, LIKE MOST OTHER SPORTS AND ACTIVITIES, takes practice if the participant expects to become proficient. Most recreational anglers, though, don't have time to juggle family and work responsibilities with an extended amount of time on the water. The outcome, generally, is an unsuccessful trip to the lake, which can lead to disinterest. Enter *Bassmaster*.

Thanks to the willingness of BASS pros to share the knowledge they have gained through countless hours of competitive fishing on multitudes of different bodies of water across the country, the learning curve for the average angler can be significantly reduced. Each chapter of this book is dedicated to a single subject or aspect of bass fishing. Each tip and pointer included in the following chapters is handed down from a pro on the Tournament Trail that has had marked success using a particular tactic, lure or pattern.

You will learn jig secrets from the nation's best jig fishermen — Denny Brauer and Ron Shuffield. Robert Lee, winner of the last four BASS events held on the California Delta, a world-renowned West Coast tidal fishery, discusses tidal water patterns. Crankbait strategies are detailed by veteran crankers Rick Clunn and Mark Davis. Noted power fisherman Kevin VanDam offers advanced spinnerbait tips. Basically, you will read how the best anglers in the nation fish their go-to baits, and how they have successfully responded to seasonal and structural patterns under every conceivable condition.

Consider this book a cheat sheet for successful angling. Thumb through the pages as though you were going through your crankbait box looking for a diver that would reach 10 feet — select the chunk of information that applies to the conditions you are facing and put it to use. Study the following pages and commit to memory the tips lying herein, and you will most assuredly turn those unsuccessful days on the lake into splendid memories — and perhaps find yourself on the water a little more often.

Copyright 2003 by BASS

Published in 2003 by BASS
5845 Carmichael Road
Montgomery, AL 36117

Editor In Chief:
Dave Precht

Editor:
James Hall

Managing Editor:
Craig Lamb

Editorial Assistant:
Althea Goodyear

Art Director:
Rick Reed

Designers:
Laurie Willis, Leah Cochrane,
Bill Gantt, Nancy Lavender

Illustrators:
Chris Armstrong, Shannon Barnes,
Lenny McPherson

Photography Manager:
Gerald Crawford

Contributing Writers:
Wade Bourne, Mark Hicks,
Bruce Ingram, Michael Jones,
Bob McNally, Steve Price,
Steve Quinlan, Jeff Samsel, Louie Stout,
Tim Tucker, Don Wirth, Jack Wollitz

Contributing Photographers:
Charles Beck, Wade Bourne, Soc Clay,
Gerald Crawford, Tom Evans,
James Hall, Mark Hicks, Bruce Ingram,
Michael Jones, Bill Lindner,
Peter Mathiesen, Bob McNally,
Dave Precht, Steve Price, Steve Quinlan,
Jeff Samsel, Louie Stout,
Gary Tramontina, Tim Tucker,
Don Wirth, Jack Wollitz

Copy Editors:
Laura Harris, Debbie Salter

Manufacturing Manager:
Bill Holmes

Marketing:
Betsy B. Peters

**Vice President &
General Manager, BASS:**
Dean Kessel

All pro profile statistics were pulled
4/13/03. Monies or titles won thereafter
are not included.

Printed on American paper by
R.R. Donnelly & Sons Co.

ISBN 1-890280-01-1

GRABBING THE LOWER LIP of a bass before dawn burns off morning's fog, has a sense of perfection about it. The contents of *Top Techniques Of The BASS Pros* is sure to allow anglers a grasp at perfection a bit more often.

CONTENTS

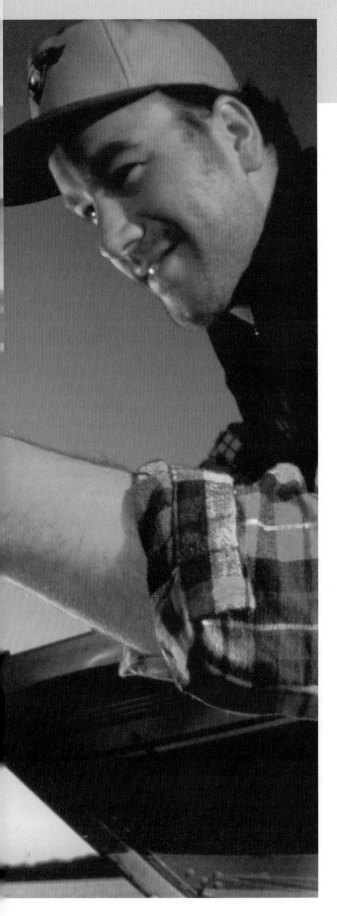

LURES

An angler's achievements
can be defined
by the tools he uses . . .

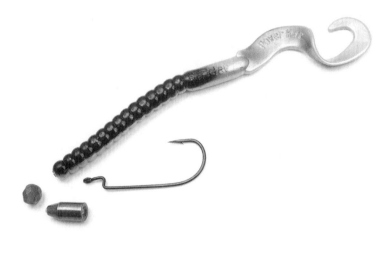

A LAYMAN'S GUIDE TO TOPWATER BASSING
A refresher course in using surface lures

TOPWATERS! THEY'RE THE most exciting of all bassing baits. Topwaters turn
fishermen into hunters, allowing them
to stalk and tantalize their prey. Topwaters also
allow their users the sensory rewards of seeing
and hearing strikes. These up-close-and-personal
lures foster one of the oldest, finest traditions in
this sport.

But beyond this, topwaters are also highly effective baits, more so than many latter generation
anglers realize. Bass blast topwaters for two reasons: to feed, and out of reflex. So, in effect, topwaters are double-your-odds baits. If fish don't
hit them for one reason, they might for the other.

Charlie Campbell of Missouri is a veteran
BASS pro who has built his reputation around

surface baits. He is arguably the best there is when it comes to "walking the dog" with a stickbait like the Heddon Zara Spook. He can even steer the bait around stumps, logs and other bass habitat.

"I think tournament fishing has taken some of the luster away from topwaters," Campbell notes. "Tournament anglers miss the dawn and dusk periods, which are two of the best times to fish topwaters. Also, when 300 fishermen fan out on a lake, they pound the banks and shallows pretty hard, and fish in these areas get spooky. Since these are the prime topwater spots, these baits usually aren't too productive in tournaments.

"But you go back to that same lake on a day when the pressure's not so heavy, and fish topwaters at the best times, and they're likely to be the most productive of all baits. Bass just naturally feed on the surface. So topwaters still play a real important role in bass fishing. Also, on a percentage basis, they're probably the best baits for catching big fish."

However, lumping all topwaters into one category is like combining all subsurface baits into another. Surface lures should be divided into "families," since each is designed for its own special purpose.

It makes sense, then, to examine these topwater families individually. Following are guidelines on when to use which, and the best tackle, retrieve methods and presentations for each. In each category, the advisor is an angler who is noted for fishing that particular type lure with finesse and success.

STICKBAITS

This deadly topwater style has the ability to excite bass in water as cold as 45 degrees, according to top BASS pros. Cigar-shaped and simple in design, these lures require a fairly high degree of skill to use properly. They are best fished by "walking the dog," a slack-slapping retrieve that causes the lure to jump to the left and right in an erratic, darting motion, highly suggestive of a panicked baitfish. Stickbaits are heavy lures and can be cast long distances, making them ideal for fishing over main lake structure, such as points and humps in clear reservoirs.

> **Bassmaster Tip**
>
> The right rod and line are essential for obtaining the desired action from a stickbait. Many pros prefer a 6-foot medium action baitcasting rod and 12- or 14-pound mono line. Line that's too light will make the lure swing too actively when you "walk" it, often causing the hooks to tangle in the line. Overly heavy line will make the lure behave sluggishly when you try to walk it.

Pro Profile
CHARLIE CAMPBELL
Hometown: Forsyth, Mo.
Birthdate: 3-5-1933

BASS Career Highlights
Tournament Titles: 1 (1974 Chapter Championship)
Times in the Classic: 5
Times in the Money: 67
Total Weight: 4,163 lbs., 10 ozs.
Career Winnings: $208,839.40
Avg. Per Tournament: $911.96

Topwater guru Charlie Campbell refined the art of "walking the dog" during his three decades of competing on the pro trail. Capable of steering a stickbait around stumps, logs and other habitat, he is arguably the best there is at the technique.

Does Topwater Color Matter?

Bass anglers have posed this question for decades: "If a bass strikes a topwater lure because of the commotion it makes on the surface, then why would its color matter?"

In theory, it shouldn't. But in reality, a topwater lure's color can make a great deal of difference, expert bassers agree. Here are some tips from guides and pros for choosing colors in topwater lures:

■ In clear water on a sunny day, a topwater lure with a highly reflective chrome or foil finish usually works best. But in clear water on a cloudy day, a surface lure with a flat finish such as black or bone often draws more strikes. Reflective colors mirror the grayness around them on a cloudy day and are harder for bass to see.

■ In murky water, help the bass find your topwater lure. Stick to dark colors (they provide the most contrast) and make your topwater bait a noisy one — like a buzzbait, prop bait or chugger.

■ At night, a black topwater lure is your best choice. To a bass looking upward, a black lure silhouettes clearly against the night sky, which is never totally black.

■ Smallmouth bass in clear lakes seem particularly attracted to a hot-colored surface lure, especially chartreuse or yellow.

■ If bass in clear lakes "park" under your topwater lure or flash on it but refuse to strike it, try using the same lure style in a more realistic color pattern — silver or gold is usually a safe choice — or take the opposite route and switch to a hot color to provoke a reaction strike.

BUZZBAITS

Virtually every spinnerbait manufacturer also makes a buzzbait. These safety-pin lures feature one or two large buzzer blades that rotate when the lure is retrieved on the surface, creating a loud sputtering noise. Buzzbaits aren't totally weedless, but their design makes it possible to fish them where most topwaters can't go without hanging up, such as over partially submerged logs and through thin emergent grass. They're also ideal around shallow stumps, blowdowns, bushes and subsurface grassbeds. Often the strike occurs when you bump the buzzer into the cover. Buzzbaits are considered big fish lures by many BASS pros. A long rod is advised; this can help keep your line off the water and prevent it from tangling in the cover you're fishing.

USE TWO DIFFERENT categories of topwater lures when fishing with a buddy to determine if the fish want a fast or slow presentation.

> **Bassmaster Tip**
>
> Don't use a rod that's too stiff when fishing a buzzbait. If you do, you may overreact and pull the lure away from the bass when it strikes the lure. A medium action rod has enough give to the tip to allow the bass to inhale the buzzer before you can react.

SURFACE WOBBLERS

These classic lures feature either a metal lip at the head (the Jitterbug, for example) or metal "wings" at the sides (Crazy Crawler), both of which cause the bait to crawl on the surface with a noisy, erratic wobbling action. They work best in low light conditions and are considered by many Bassmasters to be the best of all topwater lures at night, especially in natural lakes and ponds. Cast them around grassy shorelines and close to lily pads and weedlines for explosive strikes. Surface wobblers are noted for catching huge bass, so use a heavy baitcasting outfit and 15- to 30-pound line when fishing them.

Bassmaster Tip

Most artificial lures work best when retrieved in a stop-and-go manner, but not a surface wobbler. Retrieve it slowly and steadily — this gives the lure the profile of a swimming terrestrial creature, such as a mouse, and allows the bass to track it down easily in low visibility conditions.

TOPWATER LURES are designed to elicit a reaction strike by imitating a wounded or fleeing baitfish. Some topwaters make noisy splashes, while others silently glide across the surface.

POPPERS

These baits differ from most lures in the topwater genre because they have the ability to be worked in a confined area for a long period of time. Many anglers find that repeatedly popping one of these noisemakers over a submerged grassbed or stump can eventually irritate a reluctant bass into striking. Poppers are probably the topwaters used most often by BASS pros. Many have a streamlined profile that allows them to be cast long distances, even in the wind. Most have a bucktail or rubber skirt for a tail dressing; this gives the lure added attraction and provides some movement even when it's sitting still between pops. Some are designed to "spit water" when popped, further attracting the attention of bass. Use a 6 1/2-foot medium action spinning or baitcasting outfit when fishing poppers.

Bassmaster Tip

When fishing a popper in relatively open water, attach a piece of mono 8 to 12 inches long to the rear hook and tie a small white leadhead grub with a 1/16-ounce head at the end. When cast into a school of surfacing bass, it's often possible to catch two fish at once on this rig.

CHUGGERS

A cross between a stickbait and a popper, chuggers have a dished-out nose that creates a loud gurgle when the bait is jerked. These lures are ideal for active bass, and they draw aggressive strikes when worked fairly rapidly in shallow flats and pockets over milfoil or hydrilla, as well as on main lake points. Chuggers require a long rod with plenty of tip action to work them properly.

A STEALTHY APPROACH is critical for topwater success when prowling the shallows. Make the lure, instead of yourself, the attention grabber for the fish.

may strike a prop bait when it's reeled straight in, the best bet is to use a jerk/rest/jerk retrieve. Allow the lure to rest on the surface for a varying length of time between jerks; many strikes occur when the bait is sitting still. Be sure to check your line frequently for abrasions when using a prop bait, since the propellers can nick the line when the bait is cast.

PROP BAITS

These noisy surface baits have a propeller at one or both ends. The prop churns the water when the rod tip is jerked. They are among the best topwaters to use in choppy water or in extremely low light conditions, especially when it's raining. Although bass

USE NOISY topwaters like prop baits in the wind and stickbaits in calm conditions. The action imparted by the lures will be in sync with the water conditions.

FLOATING MINNOWS

These standby surface lures are among the best selling of all bass baits and will produce from early spring through late fall. When a floating minnow is worked with sharp movements of the rod tip, it dives a foot or so beneath the surface, hence the nickname "twitchbait." Many of these lures are made of balsa; use a long, light action rod and light line for good castability. The lifelike darting/twitching action is best achieved by attaching the lure to your line with a crosslock snap or loop knot. Like a live baitfish (and unlike most other topwater lures), a floating minnow has a subtle, quiet action, making it most effective in clear, shallow water. Cast it around flooded bushes, over the tops of submerged weedbeds and around steep rock banks.

> ### Bassmaster Tip
>
> *In deep, clear smallmouth lakes, a floating minnow is deadly in late spring and fall. After the spawn, fish it at the edges of main lake spawning flats; bass will rise out of extremely deep water to nail it. In fall, twitch it slowly at the ends of slow tapering points or "deadstick" the lure on windblown bluff banks by allowing the bait to wash back and forth in the waves on a slack line.*

BASS USE SURFACE vegetation for cover when ambushing baitfish, making topwaters prime lures for drawing the fish into open water to strike the bait.

WEEDLESS TOPWATERS

These baits can crawl right over the top of the thickest weeds without hanging up. They're practically the only artificial lures that can be successfully fished on top of thick lily pads, matted hydrilla or milfoil and pond scum. BASS pros like these baits in hot weather on shallow flats and pockets where lunkers lurk beneath thick surface weeds. The combination of big bass potential and superthick vegetation mandates a long, heavy action baitcasting rod or flipping stick and heavy line when using these artificials.

> ### Bassmaster Tip
>
> *Dense surface weeds are low visibility conditions for bass, and many missed strikes occur when you're fishing weedless topwater lures. Use a slow, steady retrieve, allowing the bass every opportunity to track down your lure. When a bass blows up on the bait and the lure disappears from view, don't set the hook immediately. Instead, lower the rod tip, count to three and set the hook hard. If the hooked bass tangles itself in thick pad stems or grass, don't try to force it out with rod pressure, or you may rip out the hook. Instead, keep a tight line and move your boat to the fish; a push pole may be necessary in the thickest grassbeds.*

CRANKBAITS ARE designed to run at specific depth ranges, from shallow to midrange and deep. The depth of the water and the type of cover found on the bottom are two determining factors for choosing the right crankbait.

A YEAR-ROUND CRANKING SYSTEM
When times get tough, Davy Hite ties on a crankbait

SINCE WINNING THE 1999 Bassmaster Classic with a Texas rigged soft plastic bait, Davy Hite has become known as a heavy cover expert — a master of flipping and pitching.

Fishing fans have likely forgotten that the past BASS Angler of the Year from Prosperity, S.C., nearly won the 1996 Classic on Alabama's Lay Lake by cranking deep, offshore structure.

The reality is that Hite is an excellent all-around angler, equally adept at finessing a floating worm as he is pitching a jig or slow rolling a spinnerbait.

The technique of cranking is the one that holds a special allure for this talented BASS pro.

"I like to think of myself as a versatile fisherman," Hite says. "I like to do whatever a particular body of water dictates. We fish a lot of man-made lakes that go hand-in-hand with crankbaits. I feel comfortable with that type of fishing."

Although he caught more than 30 pounds in the 1996 Classic by deep cranking — and came within a single pound of ruining George Cochran's celebration — Hite is equally proficient at putting a crankbait through its paces around shallow cover. He is the complete crankbait fisherman.

"I probably fish a crankbait more in shallow water, from zero to 10 feet, than in deep water," Hite adds. "But in '96, I proved I could fish a crankbait on deep structure as well. I beat some pretty good crankbait fishermen in that tournament, including David Fritts, Gerald Beck and Gary Klein."

During his frequent seminars on the art of cranking, Hite emphasizes the need to get familiar with each crankbait before ever going on the water. He spends countless hours casting and retrieving in the family swimming pool and in clear water areas of lakes. His goal in doing that is to learn the action of each bait, how it reacts after colliding with an object and the exact depth each crankbait achieves. That has helped Hite develop an impressive cranking system that has few limitations.

"I really like fishing crankbaits around wood and rock, if I have a choice," he says. "But you also need to know how to fish a crankbait in grass. I've caught my biggest stringers fishing hydrilla with a crankbait.

"A lot of people avoid fishing a crankbait around grass or brush because they are worried about hanging up. That's where practicing in clear water comes into play. You can learn how to avoid getting hung if you can see your bait swimming into a piece of cover and note what happens when you pause the bait.

"One of the biggest things is realizing when your line is hitting something during the retrieve. If you throw over a log or stump that's underwater, pay close attention to your line; it will warn you long before your bait ever gets to the object. By feeling my line rubbing against an object, I know that when my bait stops or makes contact with something, it's in some kind of cover. Knowing when you're about to come into contact with something means a lot, because it gives you time to prepare."

Hite recommends that novice crankbait fishermen use a sensitive graphite rod while learning the basics of cranking cover. The extra-sensitive rod helps them detect everything that happens to the crankbait during the retrieve.

In Hite's crankbait system, there is a role for both plastic and wood divers. When cranking around rock and gravel, he primarily uses a

Pro Profile
DAVY HITE
Hometown: Prosperity, S.C.
Birthdate: 5-18-1965

BASS Career Highlights
Tournament Titles: 5 (2001 Louisiana Tour Pro, 2001 Michigan Tour Pro, 1999 Bassmaster Classic, 1996 Alabama Top 100 Pro Division, 1994 Alabama Invitational)
Times in the Classic: 8
Times in the Money: 56
Total Weight: 2,988 lbs., 7 ozs.
Career Winnings: $823,000
Avg. Per Tournament: $7,550.46

Davy Hite's crankbait skills were honed on Carolina bass fisheries, where contrasting bottom contours make an excellent classroom setting for fishing lipped baits from shallow to deep water.

variety of lipped and lipless lures in the Japanese-made Yo-Zuri line, but he switches to more buoyant balsa crankbaits for vegetation and dense brush.

One of the intriguing elements of Hite's cranking program is his reliance on a small, homemade crankbait that has produced consistently for him over the past decade.

"It's a bait a fellow in South Carolina used to make," Hite explains. "It was called the Charlie-O, and it was sort of a secret bait that not many fishermen could get their hands on. Confidence plays a big role in fishing, and this lure became my confidence bait.

"Then when you build a bait for yourself or your friends, you have a little pride involved, too. I guess

DAVY HITE nearly won the 1996 Bassmaster Classic by cranking spotted bass ganged up on a tiny stretch of an underwater ridge, where the bottom was especially firm.

I have so much confidence in it because I've thrown it so much — now I know exactly what it will do. And what it does so well is come through cover. It catches fish in the kinds of cover that most people avoid with a crankbait."

When fishing down to 5 feet, Hite most often utilizes his homemade cranker. For middepth cover (6 to 10 feet), he switches to Yo-Zuri's Crank'N Dive model R292. For depths more than 12 or 13 feet, Hite uses a variety of lures, including Yo-Zuri's deepest Crank'N Dive (model R350), Norman's DD22, Bomber's Fat Free Shad and Mann's Deep 20+.

When it comes to crankbait colors, Hite keeps it simple. He relies primarily on two color schemes: crawfish and shad.

Most of his cranking is done with 10-pound-test Trilene XT line. With shallow cover in off-colored water, he switches to 15-pound-test Big Game monofilament. That line is propelled by

Crankbait Categories

Flat-sided crankbait

POTBELLY DIVERS

This popular crankbait style has a profile resembling a bluegill, but might also be mistaken for a crawfish or shad by a hungry bass. Its wide wobble makes it the crankbait style favored by many BASS pros for active bass in warm water, but they may also be used in cold water if the retrieve is slowed considerably. The length of its lip helps determine how deep a specific potbelly diver will swim. Most lure manufacturers offer them in the following depth capabilities:

■ **Shallow divers** — These have short, stubby diving lips capable of taking them to depths of only 1 to 3 feet. They're most effective on mud or gravel banks with sparse cover; with their short bills, they are likely to hang up when fished too close to stumps or brush.

■ **Medium divers** — These have bills longer than those on shallow divers, but not as long as the lips on deep divers. They generally run from 4 to 6 feet deep. The added bill length makes them capable of glancing off wood and rocks with a minimum of hang-ups.

■ **Deep divers** — The long bills on these popular baits will take them to depths of 7 to 15 feet, well within the range of active bass in most fishing situations. The bill also gives these lures maximum cover-deflecting capability; don't be afraid to bump them off stumps, rocks and brush.

■ **Magnum divers** — If you want your crankbait to dive deeper than 15 feet, this is the style to use. Its extra-long bill causes the lure to dive nearly straight down and provides superb deflection off deep rocks and stumps.

Potbelly diver

Jerkbait

Lipless crankbait

Metal-billed crankbait

Critter crank

FLAT-SIDED CRANKBAITS

These slim shallow divers have an extremely tight wiggle and are recommended in cold water for less active bass, as well as in dense cover. Because they do not swing in a wide arc when retrieved, they're surprisingly resistant to hang-ups and can be fished through fairly thick logjams and brush.

LIPLESS CRANKBAITS

This flat-sided bait is extremely popular for its ability to call active bass from a wide area. These shallow runners have compressed sides and most are filled with fish-attracting rattles; few lures are noisier. They're designed to be "burned" at a fast clip to attract active bass and are useful for covering a wide area of shallow water, such as a big stump flat, quickly. Although they lack a deflecting lip, the pointed nose allows them to bump off cover surprisingly well.

METAL-BILLED CRANKBAITS

Before plastic and Lexan lips became the gold standard, all diving crankbaits were equipped with metal bills. Today's versions are among the deepest of all crankbaits; many are capable of reaching 25 feet. They're ideal for bumping rocks — the metal bill is far less likely to shatter upon impact than a lip made of plastic.

JERKBAITS

Internationally, these baits number among the best selling of all fishing lures, for they'll catch virtually anything that swims. Some have shallow diving lips and float at rest; pros prefer suspending models or ones they've modified to achieve neutral buoyancy. When jerked sharply, they dive a foot or two under the surface, then pop back up again if the line is allowed to go slack. In cold weather, go with long-billed jerkbaits that dive several feet beneath the surface and hover at that depth when allowed to rest. Both styles are highly effective in clear, shallow water in reservoirs, natural lakes and streams. Most effective when fished on light line with a wire snap or loop knot. On sunny days, use reflective chrome or foil finishes; switch to bone-white or chartreuse under overcast skies.

CRITTER CRANKS

Resembling live crawfish, caterpillars, frogs, tadpoles, minnows or grubs, these small but deadly shallow diving cranks are ideal stream or pond lures. Fish them on 4-pound line using an ultralight spinning outfit. In clear water, use natural colors; try brighter colors in stained water.

either a 7-foot medium/heavy Daiwa fiberglass or graphite/glass composite rod teamed with a high speed 6:3.1 gear ratio Daiwa reel. Hite opts for a medium/heavy 6-foot rod when casting to targets in shallow water.

Like many pros, Hite has experimented with various ways of altering and weighting diving plugs. Instead of drilling, shaving or weighting crankbaits, Hite recommends you simply become more familiar with the baits in your box.

"It's more important to mark your crankbaits so you know what each one does well," Hite explains. "I will find one — whether it's plastic or wood — that will be different right out of the package. It will suspend or float a little more or sink a little faster.

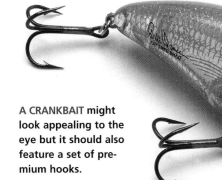

A CRANKBAIT might look appealing to the eye but it should also feature a set of premium hooks.

BLUFF BANKS where deep and shallow bottom contours merge near a river channel are prime areas for cranking. Work both sides of the structure to see which side the fish are congregating.

The ones that do something different are identified and put aside so I can play around with them later.

"Those odd baits will really pay off down the road. If I find one that suspends, I know it's a little bit heavier than the others. If I have a piece of cover I can't quite touch with one bait, I'll pull out the suspending bait. Sometimes, if I'm fishing a place with a bait that rattles and I suddenly quit getting bites, I'll switch to the quiet version. I put an 'X' on them or write 'no' or 'yes' to identify each individual crankbait.

"David Fritts goes through hundreds of baits to get those certain odd ones that really work."

In his seminars, Davy Hite goes out of his way to emphasize that deep cranking takes a special breed of anglers. Hardy, well-conditioned anglers, that is.

"It's the hardest technique I've ever learned," he admits. "It's hard on you physically, and it

takes extra concentration because you can't see what you're doing. You can learn topwater fishing quickly because you can see to do the right things. But deep cranking is all about feel."

Knowing how deep your bait will run and determining the depth of the cover that's holding bass is the first step. If you don't know exactly how deep your bait runs, there's no way you're going to get down to where you need to be, he says. The other element involved in deep cranking is being able to hit the cover you're fishing — not digging into it or riding high above it. Unfortunately, most people throw a crankbait out and wind it in without hitting anything. They avoid getting hung up, but they don't catch fish, either.

"A lot of people take the bait out of the package, find 20 or 25 feet of water and flail away," he notes. "They want to be an expert crankbait fisherman, but their baits never touch bottom. They never touch a stump, and they never get a bite. Their arms get tired, so they lay the crankbait down and go back to their old, trusty worm. They lower the worm to the bottom or into cover and catch a fish. That's enough for them to give up on crankbait fishing."

Succeeding at deep cranking requires determination as well. Simply casting and retrieving is usually not enough to coax reaction out of schools of bass utilizing offshore cover.

"You learn to do different things to create strikes," Hite explains. "At times, I've had to make 15 or 20 casts to a stump on an offshore flat before I could get a strike. There's no great secret to provoking a strike. Sometimes you have to speed up after hitting cover to get a strike; other times, you have to stop it. You just have to try different things."

The angle at which your bait hits a target is important, too.

"The first BASS tournament I won on (Alabama's) Lake Eufaula is a good example. I found those fish in practice on structure and made some casts to them, but didn't get a bite. Then I moved my boat around and made a cast from the opposite direction — and I got a bite on every cast. Those fish were there, but the bait needed to come through that structure from a different direction."

When it comes to the entire spectrum of crankbait fishing, Davy Hite has developed an understanding of its most intricate elements. Although his biggest career moment hinged on his techniques for fishing a soft plastic lure, crankbaits have remained his confidence baits throughout his entire professional life.

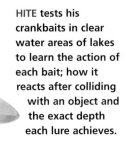

HITE tests his crankbaits in clear water areas of lakes to learn the action of each bait; how it reacts after colliding with an object and the exact depth each lure achieves.

ADD A PAUSE to your crankbait retrieve. Oftentimes, a stop in the bait action will trigger bass to strike.

SHALLOW CRANKING MAGIC
There are always a few bass in shallow water

EVERYONE KNOWS WHERE TO FIND George Cochran during a BASS tournament, but getting there is another story. The soft-spoken Arkansan believes no water is too shallow for him to fish, which is why you find him in places you'd swear were impossible to reach.

"Largemouth are shallow creatures, and you can always find at least a few fish real shallow any time of the year," he proclaims. "And if it means I've got to wiggle or push my way across a big flat to get to backwaters where they live, it's even better."

For decades, Cochran has relied on plastic worms and spinnerbaits to catch his shallow bass. And while they remain an important part of his arsenal, the crankbait has become his go-to lure in recent years.

"In times of drought, the lakes we fish become clearer than normal," he explains. "Unless there are clouds, bad weather or wind, it's difficult to catch shallow fish on spinnerbaits on a sunny day in clear water."

Spinnerbaits, he says, must be fished more slowly than crankbaits — therefore, fish get too

good a look at them in clear water.

"You can vary the speed on a crankbait and move it fast enough to trigger strikes under a multitude of conditions," he explains.

Color matters, too, especially in clear water. He opts for those that best resemble the shad, although he does like a little chartreuse on the body for darker water.

The two time Bassmaster Classic champion and other pros helped develop two Strike King crankbaits designed specifically to perform well around shallow wood. He's pleased with the results.

"You'll hang up sometimes, but not nearly as often as you might think," he says. "The key is to finesse the lure through the cover and make sure you're using the right type of lure."

Cochran says most anglers cast past logs or stumps and try to bring the lure alongside the cover. He will cast past the object and ram it into the cover.

"The best way to trigger a neutral bass is to allow that bait to bang off a log or stump," he describes. "The change in direction or action will prompt a bass to strike a lure that it might otherwise ignore. That momentary pause of the lure after it hits an object brings out the predatory instincts in bass."

Round-bill crankbaits tend to dive faster and deeper and will hang up more often than square-bill divers, he adds. The round-bill crankbait doesn't deflect away from the cover either.

"That is extremely important in my fishing, and it's why I wanted Strike King to develop the

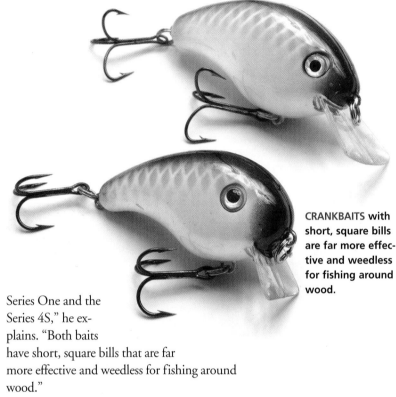

CRANKBAITS with short, square bills are far more effective and weedless for fishing around wood.

Series One and the Series 4S," he explains. "Both baits have short, square bills that are far more effective and weedless for fishing around wood."

The Series One is a small bait that runs about 2 to 4 feet deep, while the 4S has a bigger body and runs slightly deeper.

Pro Profile
GEORGE COCHRAN
Hometown: Hot Springs, Ark.
Birthdate: 5-3-1950

BASS Career Highlights
Tournament Titles: 6 (1998 Virginia Invitational, 1996 Bassmaster Classic, 1995 Missouri Invitational, 1993 Oklahoma Invitational, 1992 Alabama Invitational, 1987 Bassmaster Classic)
Times in the Classic: 19
Times in the Money: 130
Total Weight: 5,438 lbs., 13 ozs.
Career Winnings: $862,576.44
Avg. Per Tournament: $3,903.06

George Cochran's impressive tournament scorecard is grounded in his shallow water bass fishing skills — among them, using crankbaits in thin water.

Crankbait Tips

■ Small, buoyant crankbaits can be worked through lily pad fields by guiding the lure's movement with the rod tip.

■ Try jigging rattling, lipless crankbaits up and down next to vertical structure like timber or bridge pilings.

■ Paint a red gill or gash on the bait to signify blood or gills.

■ Work shallow diving crankbaits in deep water by rigging them Carolina style with a heavy sinker, barrel swivel and monofilament leader.

■ Make crankbaits swim to the side and under surface cover by bending the line-tie eye slightly to one side.

WHEN FISHING RIVER systems, George Cochran intentionally looks for obscure areas that require extra effort to reach. He believes such areas hold more fish because they are less pressured.

Cochran says he opts for bigger crankbaits in the spring and smaller ones during summer. Since most game and forage fish spawn during the spring, bass focus on the abundance of smaller minnows, and therefore, smaller baits are more effective until fall.

But during summer, other reasons dictate the use of the smaller crankbait.

"There's not a major lake in the country that doesn't have one or two tournaments held on it every weekend," he explains. "That's a lot of fishing pressure, and the smaller baits seem to get me more bites under those conditions."

The Series One comes with a pair of No. 6 treble hooks. The smaller size is appropriate for the bait, he says, but he replaces the rear hook with a larger No. 4 Gamakatsu treble.

"If you hook a 5-pounder with those smaller hooks, it can shake its head and pull free of the bait," he describes. "Since I've started putting a larger hook on the back, I've lost fewer fish."

The larger tail hook doesn't impede the lure action; it actually helps it, he says.

"When I crank the lure through cover and stop it, the larger hook seems to give it a little more action during the pause," Cochran describes.

Fishing pressure is a factor he considers when choosing locations as well. Cochran is famous for finding obscure hot spots that are often ignored by other anglers.

WHEN COMPARED to other bass species, largemouth instinctively prefer shallow water and can be found there most of the time.

He avoids the banks lined with cover because he knows they get pounded by other anglers.

"If a bank looks like it has nothing to offer, I'll fish it," he offers. "Most reservoir shorelines have some wood on them, but it may not be visible above the water. I'll target those, looking for isolated logs or stumps that lie just off the bank. They seem to always have fish on them because no one else fishes there."

In clear water, Cochran concentrates on those "nothing" banks that lie close to a creek channel, such as near a bend.

"I've learned that bass in a clear water system don't venture far from a channel," he says. "They'll get real shallow, but they want some deeper water close by."

When fishing river systems, he purposely looks for areas off the beaten path that require extra effort for him to reach. "I know that if it's hard to get in there, it probably doesn't get fished," he insists. "River bass love to go shallow."

Although crankbaits are designed to dive, Cochran has found situations in which fishing them near the surface around heavy cover can be deadly. That's a tremendous fall technique for those bluebird days following a cold front, he says.

"One day in the middle of October, a brutal cold front that passed the day before had caused a shad kill in an area of the lake where we had been catching bass," he recalls. "The shad were flitting around on the surface, and bass were coming up and nailing them."

When spinnerbaits, crankbaits and worms weren't doing the job, he tied on a big crankbait, held his rod tip high and slowly wobbled the bait on the surface next to cover.

"I caught one of the biggest stringers I've ever caught that time of year," he declares. "It's a technique I use shallow any time a real nasty cold front passes through an area."

Cochran fishes his favorite shallow crankbaits on a fast retrieve (6:1) reel and a composite cranking rod with a limber tip and stout backbone.

"The reel helps me move any slack in the line and keep pressure on the fish," he says. "I keep the

CRANKBAITS are shad-imitating imposters that can be irresistible to bass when worked erratically in shallow cover.

rod bent, but the limberness gives when the fish pulls harder. They're less apt to pull free of the treble hooks that way."

He prefers the heaviest line he can get away with using, but he will drop down to 12-pound, green P-Line in clear water and 15-pound in darker water.

"These lures were designed to be fished on heavy line," he notes. "You get more lure movement with the 12-pound line, and I think that's important when fishing clear water."

ALL ABOUT LIPLESS CRANKBAITS
Rattling baits for grass bass

RICK CLUNN CALLS IT HIS PRIMARY TOOL for locating bass, which is a lofty status considering the credentials of the man.

The tool is the lipless crankbait, a vibrating, shad-shaped, flat-sided rattling lure that allows anglers to quickly cover water in search of active bass. For the four time Classic champion, the Rat-L-Trap is his best bird dog bait, the lure he ties on when there is ground to cover and time is short.

Although he fishes it around a variety of structure and cover conditions, the Rat-L-Trap is Clunn's weapon of choice most often for a wide variety of aquatic vegetation, ranging from submerged milfoil to vertical bulrush strands. Vegetation is where a lipless crankbait can best strut its stuff, he says.

For Clunn, lipless crankbaits know no seasonal boundaries. As long as a lake or reservoir has some type of vegetation, he will automatically fish that lure.

"The Rat-L-Trap and lures like it do several things for you," Clunn says. "You can control it over the top of the weeds with the position of your rod tip. With any submerged weedbed, the top of it will vary, and this bait allows you to make quick, easy adjustments and still keep working just above the weeds.

"Weed fishing is notorious for having what I call nonpositional fish — which means you cannot predict where the bass are going to come from. With vegetation, particularly submerged vegetation, you have to search for the fish. In a stumprow or by a stickup, you know where those fish should be holding. The Rat-L-Trap is the best bait I

(Opposite page) WHEN THERE is much ground to cover and time is running short, lipless crankbaits can be the most effective lure in your tacklebox.

know of for locating these nonpositional fish. There is no doubt that the bait draws fish to it. The noise from the Rat-L-Trap will draw fish that are buried in the weeds out to see what's going on.

"It's the one bait that you don't have to present properly to the fish."

A Clunn victory at a BASS event held one spring on Alabama's Lake Guntersville is a classic example of the allure of lipless crankbaits to grass bass.

His pattern centered on isolated patches of submerged milfoil that were 1 to 4 feet below the surface in 5 to 13 feet of water. Although a few of the bass were still spawning, most of the fish were in a postspawn mode and seemed to be holding around the edges of any bare spots on the underwater islands. Clunn conquered these spots with a 1/2-ounce gold Rat-L-Trap fished on 8-, 10- and 15-pound-test line.

The Rat-L-Trap was the right tool for the situation, a bait that Clunn could use to skirt the top of the submerged vegetation and still attract the attention of bass hiding inside it. The lipless crankbait has a bigger role in grass fishing than most anglers realize, Clunn says, but he warns that this type of fishing can be frustrating.

"If you're going to crank weeds, you have to put up with a certain amount of frustration," he explains. "You can hardly make a cast without having to either slap the bait on the water or reach up and clean grass off of it. The average guy won't tolerate it. He'll either move out away from the weeds or

BECAUSE OF ITS noise factor, a lipless crankbait can attract fish holding vertically in areas such as bridge abutments.

find a place where there are no weeds. To be successful, you have to control yourself when fishing weeds and be willing to put up with fighting them all day long. Many times it would be easier to fish a worm or a spinnerbait, but they don't usually produce the strikes the lipless crankbait does."

When working a submerged weedbed or the outskirts of a vertical wall of vegetation, Clunn emphasizes keeping the lure as close to the cover as possible. That will also increase your chance of getting hung up, but popping a bait free from the grasp of vegetation also triggers strikes from time to time.

Serious consideration should be given to the equipment involved in fishing lipless crankbaits.

Clunn once used an inexpensive 7-foot fiberglass rod, and many pros still do. Some say that graphite rods allow us to respond too quickly to a strike and often take the bait away from the fish. Too, a fiberglass rod is more flexible, making it harder for fish to throw the treble hooks of a lipless crankbait.

"The best thing ever made for fishing lipless crankbaits is the high speed reel," Clunn adds. "Its value is not in the fact that it is so fast. The real key with this gear ratio reel is that it is almost a variable speed control reel. I can really feel the bait with this type reel. I can slow the bait down and speed it up without losing that feeling. That kind of control is important when you are trying to run a crankbait just over the top of brushpiles or grass."

Clunn's choice of line size varies from situation to situation. Although he primarily uses 14- to 17-pound test, he adjusts the size of the line depending on the clarity of the water and the amount of fishing pressure in the area. In his Guntersville win, Clunn began the tournament with 15-pound line, but dropped to 10- and 8-pound line on successive days. He believes downsizing his line was a major reason he was able to continue to catch fish off the same spots.

Although Clunn swears by the lipless crankbait for fishing vegetation, he insists it is a more versatile lure than most people realize.

"I've had good success with it in the fall by repeatedly casting to boat docks," he says. "It may take 25 casts to the same dock before you get a strike, but the good thing about it is that you can follow people throwing other baits, like spinnerbaits or worms, and catch fish off the docks they just fished."

During a fall tournament Clunn fished on Texas' Lake Tawakoni, low water conditions congregated the fishermen around the lake's boat docks, creating a situation where the anglers literally formed a line to fish each structure. He watched as boat after boat struck out on dock after dock with the

more conventional lures. But when he followed the parade by making short pitch-casts under the dock, the Rat-L-Trap produced two or three strikes from beneath every pier.

"It's a reflex bait," Clunn says. "I think creatures in nature have to be tuned in to subtleties to survive. Sometimes you can change some little thing to give them a different look, and that is enough to trigger a strike."

The noisy lipless crankbaits are also good tools for jump-fishing schooling bass, as well as fishing muddy water.

For all of its benefits, a problem remains with the Rat-L-Trap and similar lures that fishermen must recognize — its poor hooking ability. The basic design of the bait works in favor of a frantic bass. When a bass is struggling, the weight of the flat-sided bait provides enough leverage to work the treble hooks free on many occasions.

The biggest danger of a bass dislodging the lure is when it takes flight. In an effort to convince the fish not to jump, Clunn immediately buries 2 to 3 feet of his rod tip after setting the hook. Although that is often not enough to stop the initial jump, Clunn has enjoyed good success in keeping the bass from making subsequent leaps — the most dangerous part of the battle.

Despite its flaws, the lipless crankbait remains a viable tool for locating and catching bass. "If a lake has vegetation in it, you had better be throwing one of these baits," Rick Clunn declares.

LIPLESS CRANKBAITS can be maneuvered through thick weeds by raising and lowering the rod tip while retrieving them.

THE BLADE DESIGN on spinnerbaits greatly affects the depth the baits run. Match the blade shape to your fishing situation.

GETTING THE MOST OUT OF SPINNERBAITS
Bladed baits are all-around lures

A T A DISTANCE, THE MODERN SPINNERBAIT doesn't seem far removed from its earliest roots in the Shannon Twin-Spin, which was produced nearly 100 years ago. Without the eye-grabbing packaging of their manufacturers, even the most knowledgeable bass angler would be hard-pressed to differentiate between spinnerbait brands placed 10 paces away.

Even though the basic safety-pin format remains the same, there are certainly pronounced differences in construction, materials and performance that make spinnerbait fishing a true learning experience. Not only does a fisherman have to be concerned with colors, skirts, blades and trailers, but with options like titanium versus standard wire.

(Opposite page) POST COLD FRONT conditions are ideal for using spinnerbaits when they are slow rolled and fished tight to cover.

Unfortunately, many anglers have trouble ignoring the sizzle enough to appreciate the steak. Too often, armed with the latest technology that spinnerbait manufacturers have to offer, a fisherman takes to the water ready for anything but certain of nothing. Instead of trying to grasp the total concept of blade fishing, many seem transfixed by the mechanics and equipment of the trade.

Not a person to shun one for the other, BASS superstar angler Kevin VanDam has proved through his ongoing accomplishments that he knows precisely which part is the horse and which is the cart. To him, bigger picture items of strategy and presentation unquestionably come before any concerns over the tools themselves.

"In a nutshell, people catch fish on spinnerbaits when conditions are real good and the strike zones are large. But that's not when I'm at my best," says the Kalamazoo, Mich., pro.

"I'm at my best with a spinnerbait when the

Pro Profile
KEVIN VANDAM
Hometown: Kalamazoo, Mich.
Birthdate: 10-14-1967

BASS Career Highlights
Tournament Titles: 7 (2001 Bassmaster Classic, 1999 New York Invitational, 1999 Texas Invitational, 1997 Virginia Invitational, 1997 Maryland Top 100 Pro, 1995 New York Invitational, 1991 BP Top 100 Pro Division)
Times in the Classic: 12
Times in the Money: 110
Total Weight: 4,656 lbs., 11 ozs.
Career Winnings: $1,163,350
Avg. Per Tournament: $8,250.71

BASS millionaire Kevin VanDam's impressive track record is punctuated by his year-round use of spinnerbaits.

Customized Skirts

You can catch bass with a spinner-bait taken right out of the package, but customize the skirt and you may catch more.

BASS Pro Kevin VanDam says some skirts need trimming or pluck-ing, depending upon the situation. For example, in stained water he prefers a bulkier and longer skirt to create a larger profile and make it easier for the fish to find. In clear water, though, he prefers a smaller profile and will trim the skirt just below the hook shank and may remove 10 to 20 of the skirt strands.

"If the water is extremely clear, I'll pull out the solid colors and leave the clear or scaly strands," he says. "In extremely stained water, on the other hand, I may put two skirts on one bait for more bulk."

VanDam reminds anglers that removing skirting material allows you to reel the bait faster without causing it to lift, whereas adding skirts slows down the lure.

KEVIN VANDAM makes subtle adjustments to spinnerbaits so he can dial into specific conditions, such as matching blade shape and size to baitfish.

conditions aren't perfect, when everyone else isn't throwing them. I feel like I can make fish react to it by using the proper presentation and picking exactly the right color combinations to trigger inactive fish that other people wouldn't catch."

Of course, it's a case of easier said than done. Not all anglers have the talents of a Kevin VanDam, but they do have the same option of throwing a spinnerbait even when the conditions are not textbook-perfect. For this perennial Bassmaster Classic qualifier, the farther a situation is from the ideal, the more he has to blend big-picture strategy with the tools of the trade.

A highly organized professional, VanDam is meticulous to a fault in keeping his own world in order. While his garage may hold tackle enough to fill a mini Bass Pro Shops, the gear he takes on the water is only that which makes sense for the prevailing conditions. Look inside his boat and you'll find a small tacklebox that holds nothing but spinnerbait components, like prerigged blade/swivel/snap combinations that can be quickly added to his lure in the heat of battle.

"To maximize a spinnerbait," advises VanDam, "you always want to be using the absolute right tool."

To a large extent, the problem with spinnerbaits is how deceptively easy they are to fish and how productive they can be when times are good.

At their best, spinnerbaits excel in warm, clear water conditions when fished around abundant cover. Or they produce in shallow, stained conditions near objects such as laydowns, bushes or docks. At their worst, spinnerbaits suffer mightily in ultraclear water, under bright skies and in calm water. Cold and dirty water below 50 degrees is just as bad.

Approaching spinnerbait situations with any degree of certainty involves both information and confidence. To VanDam, the two go hand-in-hand. Knowing that spinnerbaits can cover a broad range of conditions by changing lure components and adjusting the bait for maximum performance, the stuff that others view as marginal, he sees as an opportunity.

"If you go for a while without getting a bite — on any lure — your confidence starts to fade," he notes. "Postcold-front conditions create a situation in which many anglers feel they have to go real tight to cover by flipping or pitching. This is true because you catch fish that way. But you also can do well in those conditions by tying on a spinnerbait with Colorado or Indiana blades and really slow it down, get more vibration and bump the cover.

"It's really no different than with a crankbait or jig. You want to get it banging around wherever the fish are living and keep it there for a long time under those conditions. That's what the blade combination will do for you."

These subtle adjustments in blade combinations allow VanDam to attack different problems, often solving them with a lure that others have not

even considered. This was exactly the case when he won a BASS event on the Potomac River by slow rolling a spinnerbait around shallow cover.

"Other anglers were fishing the same areas with shallow cranks or by flipping plastics, but I discovered that the bass were actually feeding on white perch, which the spinnerbait matched exactly," recalls VanDam about a stained-water pattern that placed the fish very tight to the cover.

Spinnerbait Blades, Retrieves And Colors

The shape of its blade(s) dramatically influences the way a spinnerbait looks, sounds and feels to a bass as it moves through the water. Bass pros vary blade shape and color according to water conditions and depth of the bass.

SPINNERBAIT BLADE SHAPES

There are three different blade shapes commonly used on spinnerbaits:

1 Colorado — This is the most rounded and severely cupped of the three styles, and, because it displaces the most water, produces the maximum vibration, or "noise."

2 Willowleaf — This is the longest and most slender of the three, and it produces the least amount of vibration.

3 Indiana — This "in-between" teardrop style produces less vibration than a Colorado but more than a willowleaf.

WHICH BLADE TO USE, WHEN

In general, the murkier the water or the further visibility is reduced, the more bass rely on sensing vibrations in the water rather than seeing their prey. Conversely, the clearer the water and the greater the visibility, the more bass rely on their sense of sight when feeding and less on detecting vibrations in the water.

Use a Colorado blade in stained to muddy water, or in clear water when light penetration is very low (especially at night).

Use a willowleaf blade in clear water where visibility is high. A willowleaf blade's long, slender profile and realistic flash resembles a live baitfish.

Use an Indiana blade in stained water, or in clear water on a cloudy day.

"It was bright and flat, and I was catching most of them off laydowns, fallen trees and root systems. In this tournament, the presentation was critical. I had to have the spinnerbait going right down the log with the blades bumping against it. Every time I would come to a fork in a tree or hit a branch, I would speed up the bait, crash into that limb and let it flutter down on the other side. I was working the bait very erratically and real slow, with a lot of vibration. The bass just couldn't stand to have it that close to them. When it made a quick movement, they simply reacted to it. They didn't want to bite it, but they couldn't help themselves."

Even with something as basic as slow rolling — simply fishing a spinnerbait at a slow to medium pace around cover — VanDam pushes the envelope. Through experience and diligence, he has proved to himself what works best in certain conditions, and he doesn't waste time second-guessing himself with other options.

For example, his straightforward approach to slow rolling can be broken down into two cover categories: wood and grass. If he's fishing around timber, a tandem Colorado or Colorado/willowleaf rig is the obvious choice. If the conditions are steeper and deeper, he opts for the Colorado/willow combination. In grass cover, the choice is between a 3/8- or 1/2-ounce lure, both with tandem willows that work through grass more easily.

Regardless of the cover, the one constant in his presentation is an extreme emphasis on maintaining contact with the cover and keeping the lure just above the bass.

"If I'm slow rolling off a deep, rocky point, I will let it flutter down, occasionally tick a rock and try to keep it in the strike zone — which is the entire drop, all the way down. I can also slow roll a spinnerbait around shallow laydowns with the same basic presentation — it only takes a different lure and blade combination.

"The same thing applies with weedbeds or weedy dropoffs on the outside edges of flats. I try

KEVIN VANDAM SAYS that a highly sensitive graphite rod is key in helping him "feel" a spinnerbait through heavy cover.

to keep contact with the top of the vegetation. I let it hit the weeds, pull it free and then let it flutter down. All those little movements — the quick dart as it rips out of the weeds, the fluttering down — are what trigger them to strike. Not just a slow, steady retrieve."

Aside from just avoiding the same old steady thing, VanDam's fluttering retrieve takes real advantage of inactive fish, particularly after cold fronts — when the fish hold tighter to cover and the strike zone is smaller. And unlike competitors who may opt for short-line techniques, VanDam can still cover a lot of water.

It could be argued that a Carolina rig might serve the same purpose, yet offer a more delicately presented plastic bait.

"Yes, Carolina rigging is a finesse technique you can still fish fairly fast," agrees VanDam. "The limiting factor, however, is that you're stuck to the bottom. For sparse cover, it can be very effective. But if you're around heavy cover, especially trees and grass, where the fish can be in any depth zone

from the surface down to the bottom, a spinnerbait can cover all those zones."

Again, VanDam looks at things from a slightly different perspective. To him, covering water isn't just a horizontal equation, but a vertical one as well. No matter how others make a case for their choices, spinnerbaits retain the unique ability to plumb the entire water column, producing both feeding and reaction strikes.

More than just versatility, a spinnerbait also delivers a constant stream of information during the entire retrieve. Not only is an angler apprised of bottom and cover conditions, but he knows how well or poorly the bait itself is working. In experienced hands, these clues can be invaluable.

"I can tell when a fish is just bumping the lure, when shad are hitting the blades, when it's coming through grass, whatever. I can tell the difference between all those objects, and that comes with a lot of experience," says VanDam. "It's really important to be able to do that.

"This is one reason why I fish a graphite rod with a spinnerbait. I need to know — all the time — exactly what that lure is doing. Are both blades spinning? If there is 1/4-inch piece of milfoil that sticks to one of my blades for a second, I know it's there."

This absolute attention to detail goes right to the mental side of the spinnerbait game. A striking difference between VanDam and many others is his ability to deal with sometimes-hard-to-grasp concepts — such as confidence — in very concrete terms. Even when speaking of general issues, he doesn't deal in generalities. Rather, he finds very specific ways to enhance his confidence.

"Since most bass are positioned in junction areas — forks of limbs, clumps of grass, dock pilings and such — it's not just winding past an object. It's all about having a total feel for a bait. Knowing exactly what it's doing," says VanDam about his method of building confidence by mastering the details of presentation.

"It's precisely the same thing David Fritts is doing when he's visualizing structure and feeling his crankbait over a clay point or shellbed. I'm doing the same thing. As my lure approaches an object, the first thing to hit that object is the line in front of the spinnerbait. With a sensitive rod, I can feel that and know my bait is about to collide with that object. That's all part of the total effort — maximizing the presentation when I get the bait near cover."

Although spinnerbaits have indeed changed, despite their familiar profile, VanDam's approach to fishing these lures proves that the real differences emerge from the anglers themselves. Put the best lure in the hands of an unskilled fisherman and the results will be predictably disappointing. But match a very good angler with the same tackle, and you can expect pure magic.

KNOWING HOW spinnerbait components like blade sizes affect spinnerbait action will guarantee more bass, says Kevin VanDam.

PLASTIC WORMS: THE RELIABLE STANDBY

Worms remain the most versatile of lures

CREATURE BAITS, tube jigs sprouting oblong appendages and just about any other form of freaky-looking soft plastic lure have overshadowed the patriarch of the family.

Regardless of what comes next, the plastic worm remains the blue-collar member of the soft plastic lure family. It's a worker, a roll-up-the-sleeves-and-get-the-job-done bait. It's not for purists, like some dainty topwaters. Nor is it for casual anglers, as are spinners or lipless crankbaits. Sure, those baits catch plenty of bass, even in experts' hands, but they're no-brainers. Just cast 'em out and reel 'em back in.

In contrast, plastic worms require a certain deftness on the user's part because of where and how they're offered. These squirmy baits bust cover and root out the bass. Worms catch fish that other lures don't even come close to. They are for a time when nothing else works — or works as well — which is often.

This explains why plastic worms are the most popular, most productive baits in the history of bass fishing. In their 40-plus years of existence, they have chalked up untold tons of bass, and the total mounts daily.

Larry Nixon, without hesitation, will credit the granddaddy of plastic lures for much of the more than $1 million in BASS earnings he's banked over the years. Much of this success stems from plastic worms' versatility, he believes.

"Worms can be fished virtually anywhere and under any conditions," he says. "They can be hopped across bottom, swum at intermediate depths or slithered over the surface. They can be crawled through thick brush, punched through dense vegetation, skipped beneath limbs or docks or bumped through rockpiles. Quite simply, if a bass can get there, unless it's a cave or culvert, a worm can too."

Another reason for plastic worms' success is their naturalness. They move with a tantalizing shimmy, and when a bass crunches down on a worm, it mushes like a live nightcrawler or snake, and the fish hangs on. This means more time to set the hook than an angler normally has with baits of wood, hard plastic or metal.

So the question is, if plastic worms are that

productive and millions of anglers already use them, why dwell on the subject? Two reasons. One, a review of basics is important in any subject, fishing included. Athletic teams practice fundamentals every day. And two, the art of catching bass with plastic worms is ever evolving, and anglers should periodically update their knowledge of how to use them.

Following is a refresher course to remind anglers that plastic worms, like their cousins, come in many shapes, lengths and styles.

WORM STYLES:
WHEN AND WHERE TO USE EACH

Plastic worms come in several different styles, and this difference confuses many anglers. No doubt, virtually any worm can be used in any

Pro Profile
LARRY NIXON
Hometown: Bee Branch, Ark.
Birthdate: 9-3-1950

BASS Career Highlights
Tournament Titles: 14 (1999 Michigan Top 150 Pro, 1992 25th Anniversary Tournament, 1991 BASS MegaBucks, 1990 BASS MegaBucks, 1990 MegaBucks, 1988 BASS MegaBucks, 1987 Team Championship, 1986 Missouri Invitational, 1983 Bassmaster Classic, 1982 BASS Champs Invitational, 1982 Louisiana Invitational, 1980 Texas Invitational, 1979 Arkansas Invitational, 1978 BASS Champs Tournament)
Times in the Classic: 23   **Times in the Money:** 161
Total Weight: 7,032 lbs., 2 ozs.   **Career Winnings:** $1,521,733.60
Avg. Per Tournament: $6,393.84

Hot lures come and go, but Larry Nixon has relied on the simplicity of the Texas rigged plastic worm over the course of his two decades of success on the BASS circuit.

Ten Top Spots To Fish Plastic Worms

Plastic worms can be fished virtually anywhere bass live. However, there are special spots and/or structure types that have "worms" written all over them. Following is a list of 10 such spots, and tips for working them, as recommended by top pros on the CITGO Bassmaster Tour presented by Busch.

1 LAYDOWN TREES — Trees fallen into the water offer thick cover in which bass can hide. Hold the boat off the end of the tree, and slowly retrieve a worm through the limbs. Each time the worm crawls over a limb, give it slack so it can sink back to the bottom. Work from the root wad down the trunk and through the outermost limbs.

2 FLOATING COVER — Bass like to hide beneath such floating cover as vegetation mats and driftwood. Ease in close and flip a worm into tiny holes and pockets in the cover. Use a heavy sinker (pegged) if necessary to punch through the canopy, then jig the worm slowly beneath it.

3 GRASSLINE EDGES — Hold the boat close to the grass and cast a swimming-tail worm along its edge. Try different retrieves (straight swim, lift/drop) to see which the fish prefer. Another method for fishing a grassline is to troll the boat along the edge and flip a worm in next to the vertical wall of greenery. High percentage spots include any irregularities (points, gaps) in this wall.

4 POCKETS IN MATTED VEGETATION — Keep the boat outside the vegetation, and cast a weightless or lightly weighted worm over pockets and holes in the cover. Reel the worm rapidly into the pockets, then stop the retrieve momentarily. If a bass strikes, don't set the hook until you feel pressure as the fish swims away with the worm.

5 BOAT DOCKS — Pick a dock apart. Skip-cast a Texas rigged worm beneath piers. Pull a swimming worm parallel to the sides of docks. Flip around pilings, ladders or other objects that offer shade and/or overhead protection.

6 STUMP/TIMBER-LINED DROPOFFS — Position the boat in deep water and cast perpendicular into the shallows next to woody cover. Wait for the worm to sink to the bottom, then pull it back over the ledge with a lift/drop retrieve. Or, in standing timber, cast the worm through crotches of limbs and trunks on the largest trees, then slide the worm through the notches where the limbs grow out of the trunks.

7 FISH ATTRACTORS — Thoroughly comb brushpiles, stakebeds, tire piles and other man-made attractors with a Texas rigged worm. Then move in close and flip the thickest cover again with a larger worm.

8 BLUFFS — Move in close to a bluff and cast either a Texas rigged finesse worm or a dart-head jig and finesse worm parallel to the face of the bluff. Shake the worm down as it sinks. If it hits a ledge, pop it up, pull it, and shake it back down. Work the entire bluff with this method to catch bass holding on rock outcroppings.

9 RUN-INS — Cast a Texas rigged worm into the mouths of culverts, drains, gullies and other spots where water is emptying into a reservoir. Food also washes in at these places, especially after a rain, and oftentimes bass move to them to feed.

10 ANYWHERE YOU'VE CAUGHT BASS — Use a worm as a cleanup bait to rework spots where you've caught bass on spinnerbaits, crankbaits or other types of lures. Frequently, a worm slithered through the same area will take additional fish that were reluctant to hit the faster moving bait.

worm-fishing situation with some chance of success. However, all worm styles have specific conditions for which they're best suited. Anglers who can match worms to conditions will be more efficient with these baits. Following are guidelines for when and where to use different worm styles.

Straight-tail — The straight-tail worm is what its name implies. The tail may be truly straight or with a small, flattened paddle at the end. A straight-tail worm works better with a vertical presentation than with a horizontal. It is designed for spot fishing in deeper water with a slow jigging retrieve. When the bait is hopped off bottom, the entire body of the worm reacts with a wavy, snake-like motion. A straight-tail worm is a good choice for object-oriented bass in a nonaggressive mood.

Curled-tail — Also called the "hook-tail," this is a good general purpose worm that has a straight body and a short, single curl at the end of the tail. As the worm is pulled through the water, the curled tail has a built-in swimming action. This worm is good for both deep, vertical presentations and shallow, horizontal presentations.

Ribbon-tail — This design features a thin, single- or double-curl tail which moves through the water with a pronounced rippling action. This "swimming-tail" worm is designed for shallow, fast, horizontal presentations and bass that are actively feeding. Many experts use this worm to fish aquatic vegetation, either with or without sinkers.

Sickle-tail — The sickle-tail is another swimming-tail worm, though the tail is thicker and the worm body bulkier than on the ribbon-tail. These features cause the sickle-tail to sink slower and with more vibration than the ribbon-tail. For this reason, it is well-suited for slower retrieves, often on bottom for nonfeeding bass. Also, because of their throbbing vibration, sickle-tail worms are good for flipping and/or fishing over or through vegetation.

Tube-tail — The tube-tail worm is a straight-bodied, hollow worm with tubular tentacles on the end. It is a bottom-bouncer, and when the head of the worm is on bottom, the tail floats almost vertically overhead. A good application for this worm is fishing spawning beds.

Finesse worm — The finesse worm is a small, thin, straight worm noted for its lack of action. Finesse-fishing experts use it primarily in deep, clear water, but it will also work well around shallow structure. Owing to its small size, the finesse worm must be fished on light tackle. It has the subtlest action and appeal of all plastic worms.

HOW TO WORK PLASTIC WORMS

Selecting the right worm is the first step. The next one, perhaps more critical, is using it with the right presentation. Because plastic worms are so versatile, anglers have developed numerous retrieve methods for them. Here are short descriptions for the most effective worm-fishing methods.

Bottom bumping — This is the standby retrieve for the vast majority of worm-fishing situations. Another name would be "lift-and-drop," which is an accurate description of this method. After casting the worm, wait until it sinks to the

USE A HOOK with a gap that is about two or three times greater than the diameter of the worm.

bottom (the line goes limp). Then point the rod tip at 10 o'clock, reel in slack, lift the rod tip sharply to 12 o'clock and hold it until the worm sinks back down and the line goes limp again. Repeat this lift/drop until the worm clears the area where bass should be.

Swimming — Again, the name is an accurate description of this retrieve. Instead of allowing the worm to sink to the bottom, swim it at some intermediate depth, either in a straight pull or with a series of twitches.

You may use either of two rigs. The first is a paddle-tail or swimming-tail worm rigged Texas style.

Add the least amount of weight you can to make the worm castable.

The second rig is a 6-inch straight-tail worm threaded onto the hook so it has a crook between the eye and the bend of the exposed hook. This crook causes the worm to spiral during the retrieve. (A leader/swivel above the worm prevents line twist.) Fish either of these rigs parallel to boat docks and logs, along grasslines and over

THE SLENDER SHAPE of a plastic worm makes it the perfect bait for slipping through thick cover and penetrating the strike zone.

mossbeds. The Texas rigged swimming worm will pull through heavy cover, but the spiraling rig is not weedless, so use discretion where you cast it.

Flipping and Pitching — Flipping and pitching is for fishing the heaviest cover where bass might hide. The techniques call for a long, stout rod and heavy line (20- to 30-pound test). The worm is rigged Texas style, with the slip sinker pegged flush against the hook's eye.

Position your boat close to the target cover. Then strip enough line off the reel so the worm dangles near the reel, with extra line held in the other hand. Now, engage the reel and gently swing the worm into the target spot, releasing the extra line through the rod guides. When done correctly, the worm's entry into the water is quiet and subtle. Lower the worm into the cover, then jig it up and down two or three times. If there is

no strike, lift it out for the next flip-cast to another spot.

To make a pitch-cast, point the rod toward the target while holding the worm, on a taut line, in the other hand. Then, using the rod tip as a fulcrum, swing the worm pendulum style toward the target and allow it to pull line off the reel. This motion should be smooth and controlled, like a golf swing. Using this technique, expert pitchers can hit teacup-sized targets 25 yards away.

Doodling — This vertical "finesse" technique is custom-tailored to deep, clear reservoirs and bass that are either holding near bottom or suspended at some intermediate depth. It utilizes a light spinning or casting outfit, 6-pound line and a 4- or 5-inch, thin "doodle worm." The worm is rigged Texas style, and it is preceded by a 3/16-ounce sliding sinker and a glass bead between the sinker and worm.

There are two ways to "doodle." In deep water, lower the worm to the bottom and engage the reel. Then jiggle the worm with short, continuous jigging hops (4 to 6 inches) while trolling back and forth over the target zone. In shallow water, the technique is virtually the same, except the jiggling starts as soon as the bait enters the water, and it is kept up while the worm sinks to the bottom.

Dart-fishing — A third "finesse" method, dart-fishing utilizes the same light tackle and small worms as doodling and shaking. The primary difference is that in dart-fishing, the worm is rigged behind a small (3/8-, 3/16-ounce) jighead which has the eye sticking out the top of the head. This "weight-forward" rig yields a swimming/gliding action as the worm is retrieved. Either pull this rig with little action (do-nothing method), or shake it as explained above. Experts at finesse fishing will try doodling, shaking and dart-fishing on any given day to determine which presentation the bass like best.

Wacky-worming — "Wacky" is an appropriate description for this specialized worm-fishing method. Take a 6-inch straight-tail worm, and add casting weight by pushing a small roofing nail (head sheared off) into the head of the worm. Then im-

pale the worm on a 1/0 hook by running the point through the middle of the worm, leaving the point and barb exposed. Rigged properly, the two ends of the worm dangle loosely below the hook.

This rig is used mainly in spring to catch bass spawning in vegetation, but it can be effective at other times as well. Cast it close to beds, then either retrieve it just under the surface or let it fall to the bottom, then hop it back slowly.

Dead-worming — In clear water or when angler pressure is heavy, bass may dart away if a worm plops in from above. But given time, they will return to their original location, examine the worm and, many times, suck it in. Waiting for this to happen takes mountains of patience on the angler's part, but sometimes this "dead-worming" earns bites when no other technique will.

To dead-worm (or deadstick), cast a Texas rigged worm next to a grassy patch, stump, dock or whatever, then wait for the worm to settle to the bottom. After it hits, let it rest at least 10 seconds (20 is better!). Then move the worm very gently, and wait a few more seconds. Shift the worm once more. If there's no bite, reel it in and try another spot.

THE JIG WILL ALWAYS be considered a coldwater bait, but pros have proved it's a superb year-round lure, too.

JIG FISHING SECRETS
Here's how Ron Shuffield wins with jigs

THE DATES JUNE 10, 1989; May 11, 1991; Nov. 8, 1991; and Nov. 4, 1995, probably don't mean much to you, but they certainly were memorable to Ron Shuffield. They're the dates on which four of his first five career BASS wins have come.

Even though the victories occurred at different times of the year as well as on widely different waterways — Sam Rayburn, Bull Shoals, Grand Lake and the Arkansas River — they still have one thing in common: in each event, a jig played a major role in Shuffield's victory.

The Bismarck, Ark., pro has little trouble explaining why he relies so heavily on jigs in bass tournaments.

"The thing that makes a jig so effective is that you can present it right into the center of heavy cover, where big bass usually stay, and you can put it there very quietly without any disturbance," says Shuffield, a veteran tournament competitor who's been fishing jigs since the mid-1970s.

"Jigs are not necessarily good fish finding lures, because you seldom fish them very fast — but once you do locate bass, there's hardly a better lure to catch them. And jigs tend to attract larger bass, too."

Late spring and early summer are among Shuffield's favorite months for jig fishing; during this period, he often follows one of several fish catching patterns: looking for shallow bass in the backs of creeks, fishing far up a lake's primary river tributary, and working either surface or subsurface vegetation. Later in the summer, he often fishes jigs around deeper channel drops.

"The first pattern I look for in late spring involves

(Opposite page)
JIGS ARE a high percentage hookup bait, says Ron Shuffield.

Pro Profile
RON SHUFFIELD
Hometown: Bismarck, Ark.
Birthdate: 6-27-1956

BASS Career Highlights
Tournament Titles: 6 (1999 MegaBucks Pro, 1995 Arkansas Invitational, 1991 Oklahoma Invitational, 1991 Top 100 Pro Division, 1989 Top 100 Super Pro, 1987 Top 100 Superbass Pro)
Times in the Classic: 12
Times in the Money: 100
Total Weight: 4,554 lbs., 14 ozs.
Career Winnings: $862,696   **Avg. Per Tournament:** $5,104.71

The foundation for Ron Shuffield's successful BASS career was laid on fishing with jigs. He still relies on the trusty bait to keep him in the hunt for bass and bucks.

Pork or Plastic?

When it comes to selecting jig trailers, these days the choice basically comes down to plastic or pork.

For years, most jig fishermen dressed their favorite lure mostly with pork. Pork seemed to be the perfect trailer, as it provided buoyancy to slow the bait's descent, as well as additional action behind the jig.

But pork has some limitations, particularly during the warmer times of the year when it has a tendency to dry out. That, coupled with a concentrated effort by soft plastics manufacturers to design trailers specifically for jigs, has led to a plastics domination. That is particularly true of the so-called plastic chunk that closely resembles the venerable pork chunk.

"I've become more and more a fan of plastic chunks as opposed to pork," says Oklahoma BASS pro Kenyon Hill. "With the new plastic chunks that are available today, you can match the colors of the silicon skirts on jigs very, very closely. The soft plastic chunks give you the versatility to make the overall profile of your jig bigger or smaller, depending on the situation. And the new cuts and designs have a lot of action.

"Another advantage is that pork will sometimes wad up on the hook point and cause you to miss a fish on the hook set. But that's not an issue with soft plastic. The hook point will go right through the plastic."

Ohio BASS pro Joe Thomas still relies heavily on pork trailers in his jig system — particularly a No. 1 or No. 11 Uncle Josh pork frog.

"I like pork, especially in the cold water," he explains. "Fish hold on to it better, and it's always pliable. In cold water, plastic gets a little stiff; you don't have that problem with pork."

A PORK TRAILER is more bouyant than one made of plastic. Many pros use pork because they can control a jig's rate of fall simply by adding a larger or smaller pork chunk.

searching for late-spawning bass," explains Shuffield. "I expect to find these fish in the far backs of creeks on the lower end of a lake, because these normally are the last tributaries to warm up and have spawning bass. This pattern actually works all summer — after spawning, the fish just move into slightly deeper water in the creeks. They don't swim all the way back out to the main lake.

"I like to keep my boat in the creek channel and fish the cover on both sides," Shuffield continues. "The best cover is often willow bushes and buckbrush, and I work the water down to about 8 feet."

For this pattern, Shuffield uses either a 7/16- or 9/16-ounce jig, depending on water depth and how the bass are hitting. He uses the heavier jig for deeper cover, but if bass are hitting the lure quickly as it falls, he uses the lighter jig because it sinks more slowly. These are his two favorite jig weights, and he relies on them for nearly all fishing conditions.

If this pattern does not produce, Shuffield motors to the upper reaches of the lake and into the main river tributary, where he can fish along the bank. These bass have already spawned, but because this water tends to be off-colored, they remain fairly shallow around stumps and laydowns on either side of the channel.

"For most jig fishing, you need off-colored water," he points out. "This is how I won at Bull Shoals. I went far up the White River and found the bass holding in the flooded cedars."

Shuffield's third primary jig pattern involves fishing vegetation. He likes subsurface greenery simply because it is more difficult for his competition to fish. He won the Bassmaster Top 100 on Rayburn on submergent hydrilla, hopping his jig along the outside edge of the grass in 20 feet of water.

"Most of the time, fishing the edges of vegetation will produce more bass than trying to work the potholes within the grass itself," says Shuffield. "The key is being able to picture the edge of a grassline in your mind so you can work your jig effectively. When you're fishing 20 to 25 feet deep, the contour of the shoreline doesn't always help give you this picture. You have to keep studying your depthfinder and know what it's telling you. Learning to do that is really one of the hardest parts about jig fishing."

Later in the summer, Shuffield may try still another pattern: ripping or "snatching" a jig. With this, he makes a quick, upward sweep with his rod so the lure jumps 2 to 3 feet off the bottom. He lets it fall back to the bottom, then jumps it again.

"I like to use this on practically any type of drop that has cover," explains Shuffield, "but you need water at least 12 to 15 feet deep, such as near the mouth of a creek or perhaps off secondary points in that creek where the channel is nearby. The bass will hold close to cover, but you can make them come out of that cover with this retrieve. I think it generates a reflex action."

"Most hits on a jig come as the lure is falling, so you try to make it fall several times wherever you're fishing. Simply dragging a jig along the bottom rarely produces, and I seldom retrieve a lure that way."

Shuffield's jig-hopping technique is fairly simple. He engages the reel as soon as the jig touches the water, and he lets it fall to the bottom on what he calls "controlled slack." Then, he reels in any slack in the line so he can detect what is happening to the lure.

"Next, pop or jerk your rod lightly once or twice so the jig hops," he explains. "Don't move your rod much; when you lower it, bring it down only to about the 10 o'clock position each time. With your rod held fairly high, you'll have better contact with the jig, and you can immediately lower the rod for a better hook set. Also, you're in position to hop the jig again."

Shuffield controls the slack in his line by reeling slightly as the jig is falling after each hop. This keeps the jig moving forward, and because line bow is absent, line-watching for light strikes is easier.

"You don't ever let a jig fall on a totally slack line," Shuffield emphasizes, "because then you're not in contact with it. If a strike occurs, you won't see or feel it, and strikes almost always come as the jig is falling."

Shuffield even employs this double-hop retrieve when he's pitching or flipping into the middle of heavy cover. He lets the lure fall to the

IN LATE spring and summer, as long as the water is somewhat stained, flip jigs to bank structures on the upper end of a lake.

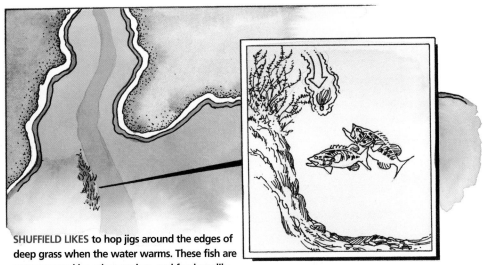

SHUFFIELD LIKES to hop jigs around the edges of deep grass when the water warms. These fish are not pressured by other anglers, and feed readily.

bottom, raises it several inches, then hops it straight up several more inches. It isn't a violent jerk at all; in fact, when he's working extremely heavy cover, his rod tip action is hardly noticeable. Again, all he's trying to do is create more falls, and he'll do this two or three times before reeling in and pitching to another target.

Occasionally, Shuffield swims a jig, particularly on lakes that have deep boat docks (especially

Jig Fishing In Summer

Bob Carnes, manufacturer of Arkie Jigs in Springdale, Ark., offers other tips for summer jig fishing, particularly in deeper water. He prefers a 1/4-ounce jig tipped with a No. 11 Uncle Josh pork chunk, using lines testing up to 17 pounds, depending on water clarity.

"One of my favorite techniques is what I call 'ticking the treetops,' " says Carnes, "and I use it when bass are suspended 25 or 30 feet down in flooded trees. The heavier lines I use let my lightweight jigs fall slower, and also help keep them from snagging quite as much, due to the water resistance on the line.

"I cast well past the target tree and let the jig fall in an arc right down over the top of the tree," continues Carnes, "so it just touches the uppermost limbs. If the fish are deeper, I let the jig fall a little longer, but basically, you treat the timber like the bottom, even though the top of the tree may be 60 or 70 feet up off the lake floor.

"Normally, you will find one or two trees that will hold bass during the summer months year after year. Finding the trees is the hard part. Look for trees out on points, different types of trees or subtle depth changes. It takes a lot of work and study, but believe me, once you find such a place, it will pay dividends from then on."

floating docks) and piers, where bass may be suspended. In situations like these, he may change to a lighter 1/4-ounce jig with a large pork trailer. He lets the lure fall about 2 feet, then swims it back along the pilings with a gradual pull-and-fall retrieve.

Another technique Shuffield emphasizes is to "fish" jigs through heavy cover rather than pull them through. Jigs can be worked through the thickest, heaviest cover if the angler is careful.

JIGS ARE THE ultimate weapon for fishing the stairstepping contours of ledges in deep, clear lakes, says Ron Shuffield.

"Again, this relates to staying in contact with the lure and feeling the branches and limbs it touches," he explains. "When you feel and see the line going taut as the jig begins to hang, don't pull it or try to force it. Instead, yo-yo it or ease it through very slowly with your rod tip. This is a good time for a strike, too, so stay alert."

To help make his jigs more weedless, Shuffield also spreads the fiber weedguard so it more effectively covers the barb.

Shuffield prefers a 7 1/2-foot heavy action flipping/pitching rod when he fishes jigs in heavy cover. He may change to a shorter 7-foot, heavy action stick when casting jigs to isolated targets like brush or standing timber. He normally uses 25-pound-test line, due to the heavy cover he prefers to fish.

"To me, the most important aspect of jig fishing is to know the lure's rate of fall and knowing when to change it," he says. "This, basically, is lure presentation. When bass are really active, they'll often hit a jig very quickly. Other times, they're more sluggish and need to look at it longer.

"Believe it or not, the slight difference in the rate of fall between a 7/16-ounce jig and a 9/16-ounce can mean a lot to a bass. In 90 percent of the cases, a slower fall is better."

Basically, Shuffield uses lighter jigs when bass are shallow; in fact he frequently uses a 1/4- or even a 3/16-ounce jig when fish are as shallow as 4 feet. On the other hand, he uses 9/16- and 3/4-ounce jigs when he's fishing deeper water or needs the jig to penetrate heavy cover. In his BASS win on Sam Rayburn, he used a 3/4-ounce jig to work through the hydrilla.

"You can also slow a jig's fall by adding a larger pork trailer, and of course, you can speed it up by using a smaller trailer," he notes. "I use pork trailers the majority

of the time because they're more buoyant than plastic, and they give me added control over the lure.

"A lot of anglers tell me they use plastic trailers in the summer and pork in the winter, but I don't think it really makes much difference. I've caught bass with plastic trailers in 47 degree water and with pork trailers in 90 degree water. I think the places and ways you fish a jig are more important."

Shuffield isn't a strong advocate of different jig colors; his tacklebox rarely has more than three or four color combinations. His favorites are black/blue and pumpkinseed/green for clear water, and black/chartreuse and brown/orange for anything else. If bass aren't hitting any of these, he'll switch to black/red, which seems to produce in dingy as well as clear water. He matches these colors with pork trailers.

"I try to keep the colors as simple as possible," he says, "and because these colors produce well for me, I don't see any real reason to change. So much of jig fishing — the color, size and even technique used — is simply a matter of confidence. Jigs are not easy to learn to use. You not only have to develop confidence in the lure but also confidence in your own ability to use it."

Shuffield began building confidence in jigs back in 1975, when he heard fishermen were catching a lot of bass at night on Lake DeGray with Bob Carnes' Arkie Jigs. He'd never used jigs prior to that time, but he and some friends started trying them, hopping the lures around shallow cover on the Arkansas lake. Before long, they were bringing in 10-bass stringers weighing more than 60 pounds, and Shuffield had become a confirmed jig user.

MOST PROS BELIEVE that jigs elicit quality strikes, and that reason alone makes them the best lure when flipping and pitching along shoreline cover.

Despite his expertise with the lure, he admits that there are many times when he doesn't know all the answers.

During the 1993 Alabama Bassmaster Invitational on Lake Eufaula, for example, he found an inviting-looking bush in shallow water that seemed tailor-made for a jig, but he couldn't get a strike. Then Shuffield snagged his jig in the bush and had to break his line.

"I trolled the boat away to keep the wind from blowing us back into it while I tied on another jig," Shuffield remembers. "Then, for some reason, I went right back to it, and on my first pitch I caught a 5-pounder.

"Now, whenever I give a seminar about jig fishing, I talk about the importance of a quiet lure presentation that doesn't disturb the water, but in this instance I could hardly have disturbed the water more if I'd tried.

"I guess that bass was just stubborn and wanted to see how persistent we were."

TECHNIQUES

Unobtrusive pitches,
delicate flips and
wake-making retrieves all work —
if you know when to use them . . .

KNOWING HOW TO find the balance between terminal tackle and soft plastics is a key to successful Carolina rigging.

ADVANCED CAROLINA RIGGING

This deep water technique works wonders year-round

WHEN IT COMES TO CAROLINA RIGGING, O.T. Fears is a star. The veteran Oklahoma pro utilized the deep water technique to break two coveted BASS records during a tournament on South Carolina's Santee Cooper lakes. He weighed in a five bass, 34-pound, 4-ounce limit, sandwiched between stringers of 28-9 and 14-7 — giving him a 77-4 total that established the new high water mark for a three day, five bass limit tournament.

Not surprisingly, Fears can be seen slinging a Carolina rig year-round to catch bass anywhere he goes and under most conditions. It is, he says, his bread-and-butter technique on the tournament trail.

"Carolina rigging is my most dependable technique," praises Fears. "I probably fish a Carolina rig 70 percent of the tournament year.

"It's such a versatile technique — probably more versatile than any other I know. I fish it a lot of different ways. Most people just put a 1-ounce weight on the line and chunk it out in deep water. They use it in the late winter and early spring for prespawn bass. But it's also a tremendous tool for fishing shallow during prespawn and postspawn, and it's great in summer, when the bass gang up on deep structure. It's a tool to be used all year long."

As a result, Fears often scores big under conditions in which others are struggling.

"What dictates when I use a Carolina rig? A combination of factors, including the prevalent cover or structure," he continues. "You have to take everything into consideration.

"A lot of it depends on the time of year, but it also depends on the mood the fish are in. A lot of times, they will bite a bait that's suspended off the bottom,

(Opposite page)
ADJUST THE LENGTH of your leader according to water depth. In shallow water, shorten the leader to 18 inches.

Pro Profile
O.T. FEARS III
Hometown: Sallisaw, Okla.
Birthdate: 12-2-1946

BASS Career Highlights
Tournament Titles: 4 (2000 Louisiana Invitational, 1995 Georgia Invitational, 1994 Bassmaster Superstars, 1994 South Carolina Invitational)
Times in the Classic: 4
Times in the Money: 65
Total Weight: 3,567 lbs., 10 ozs.
Career Winnings: $345,217.40
Avg. Per Tournament: $1,939.42

O.T. Fears is a Carolina rig slinger who has proved the bait can be used year-round and coast-to-coast with great success.

Varying Lures By Season

Pros often vary the lures they use when Carolina rigging by season. Following is a sample of what they typically use.

■ SPRING: Use smaller lures in cold water. Four-inch worms, "French fries," grubs, tube baits and plastic craws produce best.

■ SUMMER: Bigger lures get the nod. Some pros routinely use 9- and 12-inch worms in warm water. If bass don't respond to these, however, stick to 6- and 7-inch worms or 6-inch lizards.

■ FALL: As the water cools and baitfish become more active, try hard floater/diver minnow lures (jerkbaits) on a Carolina rig, especially in clear lakes. Use reflective chrome or gold patterns on sunny days for maximum flash, but switch to bone, gray or chartreuse on cloudy days. Six- and 7-inch worms and lizards also continue to produce in fall.

MORE CAROLINA TIPS

Here are some additional tips pros suggest when using a Carolina rig:

■ Keep Carolina components in a separate tacklebox. Many pros use a clear plastic utility box for sinkers, beads, swivels, etc.

■ Rattles and "clackers" (brass cylinders) that slide up your mainline, below the sinker, are available. These add more sound to your presentation.

■ Vary the sinker weight according to conditions. Some pros drop back to 1/4 ounce in clear water. A heavy sinker is usually not advised when fishing the rig around thick cover.

■ Wrap prerigged leaders around a section of board or stiff foam and keep them in your boat. This will save rigging time when you're fishing.

WEIGHTS FOR Carolina rigs come in a variety of shapes to keep them from snagging as they bump across the bottoms.

and the bait on a Carolina rig suspends better than a Texas rig or something else you drag right on the bottom.

"It works so well because it floats above the bottom. And it's a more subtle bait presentation. It doesn't move quickly. When you move it, the lure kind of sails and then settles down. That's why it will produce under a variety of situations."

Fears works a Carolina rig in cover that others wouldn't dare drag a big weight through.

"I catch a lot of fish throughout the year by Carolina rigging in heavy grass," Fears says. "A lot of people wouldn't even try throwing a 3/4-ounce or 1-ounce weight into hydrilla or eelgrass that's real thick on the bottom."

Fears has adapted some of his Carolina rig techniques to fishing heavy grass.

When fishing around vegetation, Fears uses two different variations of the bait: One sports a 5/8-ounce weight with a 1/16-ounce pointed Water Gremlin bullet weight on top of it to help penetrate the hydrilla. For thicker patches of weeds, he switches to a 1/2-ounce weight and a small Water Gremlin in front to help it bore through the vegetation. For both rigs, he uses a 3-foot leader made of fluorocarbon line, which doesn't absorb water (as much as monofilament) and is more buoyant. This enables the lure to float in the grass as it is retrieved.

His leader length depends on the height of the vegetation off the bottom. Fears usually begins with a standard 3- to 4-foot leader and then increases it a foot or two to ensure his Carolina bait floats above or near the top of the grass.

With all of his Carolina rigs, Fears uses three beads (two plastic and one glass). The glass bead is positioned in the middle of the two plastic beads to create a loud clicking sound. The bottom plastic bead protects the weight from the hard glass bead, which can eventually pound the lead flat and possibly pinch the line.

"It's a pain to fish a Carolina rig in real thick grass," he admits. "(The difficulty) depends upon the type of grass. Hydrilla is a little different because

CAROLINA RIGS ARE an excellent choice for fishing weedy breaklines because they can be fished over the top of submerged weeds.

it's more of a hard grass. It feels like a rock down there when you're bumping hydrilla. It doesn't get balled up on those light sinkers very much."

When Carolina rigging vegetation, Fears most often drags a creature bait, a lizard or a tube jig.

"One of my favorite techniques is to fish the inside grasslines like those you find at Sam Rayburn Reservoir (Texas)," adds Fears. "The hydrilla grasslines will usually be 5 to 10 feet deep. You can throw out in the open water toward the bank and pull it back to the inside grassline. Then, let it sit there and rattle the beads on the sinker. Often, you will just be sitting there holding it, and pretty soon you will feel a little tick — or the fish will just start to move off with the bait."

To gear up for Carolina rigging, Fears chooses a 7 1/2-foot medium action rod designed for crankbaiting walleye. Most pros prefer stout rods, including flipping sticks, but Fears believes a stiffer rod can cause a fisherman to lose bass that hit Carolina rigs.

The extra length enables Fears to set the hook by turning his body and sweeping the rod on a horizontal plane, which quickly takes up line and erases much of the slack inherent in this long line technique.

In his Carolina rigging system, the BASS champion sets himself apart from the crowd by utilizing several different types of weights. In addition to the traditional egg-shaped sinker, his Carolina rigging box contains cylinder-shaped Mojo-style weights in 3/4- and 1-ounce sizes for fishing deep grass and brush; Water Gremlins with pointed noses; and Lindy No-Snagg Slip Sinkers, which are elongated weights covered by a rubberized material that slips through rocks with ease.

"A lot of people won't throw a Carolina rig in shallow water, but I'll fish it as shallow as 2 or 3 feet, especially before and after the spawn," Fears says. "In shallow water, I'll shorten the leader to 18 inches and use a 1/2- or 5/8-ounce sinker. There is a short time in spring when shallow Carolina rigging really shines. But it's a great way to intercept some huge fish as they come in to spawn."

Understanding his affinity for the Carolina rig, O.T. Fears was asked to detail the times he is most likely to leave his dragging rod strapped to the front deck of his boat.

"If the fish are real active and aggressive, and they're biting crankbaits, spinnerbaits or topwaters, I'll fish something that I can work more quickly," he says. "The Carolina rig works for bass that are not very aggressive, and it's good in situations where you can't get another bait to those fish — when the fish are holding on really deep structure.

"Often, the bass will be in a subtle mood, and that calls for the subtle presentation you get with Carolina rigging. That situation is where this technique ideally matches the mood of the bass."

WHEN FISH ARE inactive and sluggish, especially in summertime, the Carolina rig is the go-to bait for BASS pro O.T. Fears.

TOOLS FOR FLIPPING AND PITCHING

Close quarters calls for a flippin' stick

YEARS BEFORE VIRGINIAN CURT LYTLE competed in BASS tournaments, he purposely tackled different types of waters and mastered a wide variety of fishing techniques. His goal was to become versatile enough to hold his own against the country's most elite anglers.

Lytle learned his lessons well. After passing the initiation that comes with being a rookie on the BASS tour, Lytle won a tournament and became a CITGO Bassmaster Classic presented by Busch finalist. In short order, he widened his angling repertoire while honing his skills at individual techniques. Even though Lytle keeps an open mind and brings a diverse assortment of tackle to every tournament, a stout flipping rod constitutes the foundation for his success.

(Opposite page) PITCHING IS preferred over flipping when a quick presentation is required to cover large areas of shoreline cover.

"My philosophy is simple," says Lytle. "If I think there are enough bass in shallow cover to keep me in the running, I'll spend a whole lot of time with a flipping stick in my hands. Sometimes that strategy hurts me, but it also has been the main reason I've done as well as I have."

Due to the amount of time Lytle wields a flipping stick, he makes a lightweight, stripped-down model to reduce the workload. Lytle credits friends Mike Watson and Gary Farmer of Johnson City, Tenn., for showing him how to construct a featherweight flipping rod. His rods are fashioned after theirs.

"A heavy flipping rod is hard on your joints and wears you down after a long fishing day," says Lytle. "That undermines your proficiency. A light rod reduces the physical stress and is also much more sensitive. It lets me feel strikes better and react to them quicker."

A 7 1/2-foot graphite blank made for inshore saltwater fishing comprises the heart of Lytle's flipping rod. It has the stiffness needed for flipping, but it is lighter in weight.

He matches the rod with a low profile baitcasting reel with a sturdy aluminum frame.

Pro Profile
CURT LYTLE
Hometown: Suffolk, Va.
Birthdate: 3-28-1969

BASS Career Highlights
Tournament Titles: 1 (2000 Missouri Invitational)
Times in the Classic: 2
Times in the Money: 23
Total Weight: 1,037 lbs., 8 ozs.
Career Winnings: $119,433.33
Avg. Per Tournament: $2,095.32

Curt Lytle has found enough bass living in shallow water to pitch and flip his way to notoriety on the BASS tour.

A LIGHTWEIGHT, stripped-down flipping stick comes in handy when Curt Lytle is making repeated casts.

A right-handed angler, Lytle flips with his right hand and switches the rod to his left after the bait hits the water. When pitching, which Lytle finds more tiring, he alternates between his right and left hand to cut down on fatigue.

"If you're digging a ditch with a shovel, eventually you're going to switch hands to give yourself some relief," says Lytle. "It took me about six months to learn to pitch left-handed. I'm glad I made the effort to do so."

When Lytle finds himself in a situation where his target is just out of flipping range, he'll grasp the rod at the very end of the butt, and flip. His light rod helps him perform this trick, which adds an extra foot or two of distance. Though pitching would easily get there, it doesn't give Lytle the supersoft lure entry and pinpoint precision he achieves when flipping.

Lytle most often flips and pitches a 1/2-ounce jig with loud rattles. Black-and-blue gets the call in stained to muddy water, while green pumpkin and watermelon fare better in clear water. Lytle dresses his jigs with a plastic chunk in matching colors.

When bass ignore jigs, Lytle switches to a large profile plastic worm with a fat, deeply ribbed body about 1 inch in diameter. When it falls, its curled tail extends and undulates, increasing the lure's length to about 6 inches.

"Most of the time you go to plastic when you want to show bass something that has a smaller profile than a jig," says Lytle. "It is smaller than a jig, but it has more bulk than any other plastic bait."

The worm often produces for Lytle after cold fronts, and when he fishes behind other anglers who are flipping jigs. Some anglers opt for lengthy worms in the same situations, but Lytle eschews such baits because they latch on to branches and other cover and spook the very bass he is trying to catch.

Lytle rigs the worm with a 1/4- to 3/8-ounce bullet sinker and a 4/0 wide gap hook. Green pumpkin, black with blue flake, and black with red flake handle any water conditions Lytle encounters.

Any shallow cover is a likely target for Lytle's flipping rod, including aquatic vegetation,

Flipping Tips

■ Flipping is 100 percent wrist action. Rely on the leverage of the rod and the pendulum motion of the swinging bait to do most of the work.
■ The importance of a silent lure entry cannot be overemphasized. A loud splash puts bass on alert.
■ Since flipping is normally done in murky to muddy water, a bulky, high visibility lure is recommended. Dark colors (black, blue, purple) are most visible in murky water. Contrasting dark colors (black/blue, red/purple) are favorites of many pros. Of course, altering the color of the jig's trailer may further refine your presentation.
■ As the lure falls, use your thumb to gently feather the spool. The lure should drop straight down, so avoid too much thumb pressure, which will cause the lure to be pulled away from its target.

windfalls, stumps, flooded bushes and docks. When fishing vegetation, preferably milfoil and hydrilla, he looks for grass adjacent to wood cover, rocks, a current or some type of edge. Current was the key during a BASS tournament on the Potomac River, in which Lytle finished in the Top 10.

"In that tournament, I fished clumps of milfoil in a creek mouth just off the main river," says Lytle. "I concentrated on grass clumps that had current pushing against them. I was using a creature bait, because the current made the bait's legs and tail work."

Water color often determines where Lytle fishes on a given body of water. Though he doesn't hesitate to flip and pitch in clear water, he opts for stained to muddy water when given a choice. He claims bass in muddy water hold tighter to cover and are more susceptible to close-quarters tactics than clear water bass.

"Say you've got a bass holding under a dock in clear water," says Lytle. "That fish may swim out several feet to nail a jerkbait, topwater plug or spinnerbait. But in stained water, that same bass won't move 2 feet from the dock to take a bait. That's when it's hard to beat a flipping stick."

Docks stationed over deep water get little attention from Lytle. He relies on his depthfinder to locate shallow docks in 3 to 5 feet of water, which he believes appeal more to bass. Bass may hold anywhere on a dock, and Lytle fishes these structures from front to back to determine the prevailing pattern. If the outside edge of a dock sits over water deeper than 5 feet or so, Lytle swims his jig or worm above the bottom to entice any bass suspended beneath the dock.

"A spinnerbait or jerkbait may be a better choice in that situation," says Lytle. "But I'd rather swim a bait occasionally with my flipping stick than fumble around switching rods. I catch a lot of bass with a swimming retrieve."

During practice rounds before actual tournament competition, many anglers search for bass with lures that comb water quickly, such as spinnerbaits and crankbaits. When the money's on the line, and they need to milk productive areas for every strike, anglers resort to a flipping rod. Lytle acknowledges the wisdom of that approach, but it's not his style.

"I'm quite comfortable using a flipping stick to locate bass in practice," says Lytle. "I may not cover as much water this way, but I know I'm not as likely to pass over bass when flipping as when I'm fishing something with a faster presentation. If there's a mess of bass where I'm practicing, I'll surely catch one."

Pitching Tips

■ With practice and a properly adjusted reel, it's possible to speed up the pitching procedure by not grasping the lure in your hand. Merely dropping the rod tip can put the lure back in motion.

■ Because pitching is used in clearer water, it's a faster technique than flipping. Once your lure has left the cover, reel it in quickly and pitch again.

■ If the water is murky to muddy but obstructions such as standing timber prohibit you from getting close enough to flip, try pitching instead.

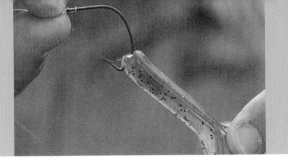

THE TINY TUBE JIG is a top shelf lure for the BASS pros.

MASTERING FINESSE FISHING
Downsize your lures when the bite is tough

IN THE LATE 1980S, when the rest of the fishing world discovered a class of bass lures that Western anglers had been using for some time, Rick Clunn elicited quite a bit of laughter by labeling them as "sissy baits."

The sissy bait reference amused a lot of people, particularly the "bubba" fisherman who knew nothing but heavy line and big baits. As a Californian then, Gary Klein (who now lives in Texas) took his share of kidding about fishing these tiny lures and light line. Sissy baits were a running joke on the Tournament Trail for a time.

But times have certainly changed. Catch a few big stringers, weigh in a trophy bass or two or win a couple of tournaments on a lure or certain technique — and you quickly create some disciples of the very aspect of bass fishing they once ridiculed.

That is a brief history of sissy baits.

These days, learning to fish light line and small finesse lures is an absolute necessity, both on and off the national tournament trail. Every angler will eventually have to learn how to use these baits if he hopes to catch fish consistently.

Sissy baits — or "finesse lures," as they are properly called — can be the answer to heavy fishing pressure because these slow and subtle baits will catch for anglers fishing behind a lot of other fishermen. They also work better than larger, faster lures in tough fishing conditions like clear water and following cold fronts.

As the years go by, fewer and fewer new reservoirs are being built in the United States. And as the lakes we do have get older, they get clearer and lose a great deal of their cover. Lakes in northern California fluctuate as much as a foot a day.

Lake Oroville, which used to be Klein's home lake, is 600 feet deep and fluctuates 95 feet a year. When this lake was created in 1966, the timber was cut, but all of the brush was left.

THE SLOW, spiraling fall of a tube jig is ideal when sight fishing for bedding bass.

Pro Profile
GARY KLEIN

Hometown: Weatherford, Texas
Birthdate: 10-11-1957

BASS Career Highlights
Tournament Titles: 8 (2003 Georgia Tour Pro, 1996 Missouri Invitational, 1993 Alabama Invitational, 1990 Florida Invitational, 1989 Texas Invitational, 1988 Arkansas Invitational, 1985 Georgia Bassmaster Invitational, 1979 Arizona Invitational)
Times in the Classic: 20
Times in the Money: 147
Total Weight: 6,131 lbs.

Career Winnings: $1,079,644
Avg. Per Tournament: $4,819.84

As a young Californian, Gary Klein staked his early reputation as a topflight BASS pro using Western finesse techniques.

GARY KLEIN uses
finesse techniques in
postfrontal conditions
to coax finicky bass
from their hiding
places, including boat
docks.

Years of erosion have had an impact. Now, the banks are virtually bare. And the water, which once was fertile and somewhat colored, is now extremely clear.

More and more fishermen are turning to sissy baits when the toughest fishing conditions exist. For example, these little baits are excellent for the days after a cold front passes through and is followed by bright skies, clear water and finicky bass. That's just another reason why, sooner or later, everybody is going to have to learn to fish these little baits.

"My definition of a sissy bait includes lures weighing less than 1/4 ounce, which can be cast on 6- to 8-pound-test line," says Klein. "I never go down to 4-pound test. I grew up fishing for small-mouth and really believe there is no difference in the number of strikes between 4- and 6-pound line. With plastic baits, anything under 5 inches in length could be considered a sissy bait.

A lot of people automatically think of these lures as dainty baits. But you can transform these sissy baits into something that is anything but dainty. You can make a 5-inch grub a "power bait"

by flipping it on 20-pound-test line and with a 1/4-ounce slip sinker. Another example would be the ultralight crankbaits, like the Bagley Honey B or Rebel Wee R, which Klein sometimes fishes on 15-pound-test line and a 7-foot glass rod. "If an 8-pounder hits that crankbait, I'm going to boat it — and if a 12-pounder nails it, I have a good chance of landing it," he declares.

Finesse fishing is as much a philosophy as it is a technique. Like any other productive method, it requires a lot of thought.

"I am the type of fisherman who is always looking for ways to get more efficiency out of a lure or find a more efficient way to work the water," he adds. "It seems like the smaller the bait that you use, the more inefficient it becomes.

"First of all, it is lighter, so it is harder to throw. And your lost-fish ratio is increased. So that's why I am constantly looking for ways to modify my tackle and the lure itself."

A prime example is those little crankbaits mentioned above. Klein modifies them by removing the tail hook completely and adding a much larger belly hook, which gives him improved hooking ability without hampering the action of the lure. The larger treble on the belly increases his landing ratio back up to the 90 percent level he strives to achieve. It's still difficult to cast, but he puts up with that flaw.

"I have spent quite a bit of time playing around with different hook sizes in a swimming pool and experimenting with hook placement," Klein notes. "That was when I found that the single hook has to go on the belly of the crankbait, where it enhances the natural buoyancy of the lure. The single treble hook tucks under the body of the bait, allowing me to walk it through standing timber, like you would a much larger crankbait."

It is important to put some thought into these sissy lures — not only crankbaits, but jigs, grubs and plastic worms.

"Even though I'm forced to downsize my baits at times, I still can catch big bass," Klein says. "I know there is always the possibility of a quality bass hitting finesse lures, so I don't compromise in hook size. I might drop down to a 1/8-ounce slip sinker, but I still want a strong 2/0 or 3/0 hook."

In Klein's sissy bait arsenal are several lures the average angler probably doesn't consider to be finesse baits. The little crankbaits are a good example, but others include 1/8-ounce spinnerbaits, small lead spoons and in-line spinners.

The spinnerbait, which has a small (No. 1) Colorado blade, is fished on 8- to 10-pound line and a baitcasting outfit. Like most of his smaller baits, it is especially effective in September and October, when bass are very oriented to creek channels and are conditioned to feeding on small minnows and bass fry.

He is most apt to fish the little crankbaits in a natural body of water like Albemarle Sound or the James River.

"I fish it like you would most spinnerbaits — throw it into the junk and walk it back out. These lures are most effective when you 'bump the stump' with them," he notes. "I used these small diving plugs

to catch several bass off cypress trees in the James during the 1990 Bassmaster Classic. These lures were a good choice there, because I was fishing heavily pressured areas, and bass were accustomed to the small shad prevalent at the time."

While most anglers who fish small crankbaits cast them on spinning tackle, Klein prefers a 7-foot fiberglass rod and baitcasting reel. Obviously, casting lightweight lures on a baitcast rig requires plenty of skill.

"One important aspect of combining sissy baits and heavy tackle is it really takes a lot of practice and experience to get in tune with the lure," he adds. "You need to spend a considerable amount of time both on the water and at a swimming pool

MINICRANKBAITS are most effective in heavily pressured areas where the jaded fish reject large lures.

my spinning outfit around boat docks, pilings, vertical bluffs and long points, I prefer the ultra-light version.

"I concentrate on giving the spoon action as it falls to the bottom and then as I work it back to the boat. Most strikes come on the initial fall or subsequent flutter."

One of his most productive finesse tools for smallmouth bass is a small in-line spinner. Using 6- to 8-pound line, he fishes it around gradually sloping flats littered with boulders — places where smallmouths often spawn. These bass usually prefer downsized lures, and in-line spinners have the flash of a spinnerbait, yet are diminutive.

Those are some of the more unorthodox sissy baits. But Klein's bread-and-butter finesse lures are plastic worms, tube jigs and grubs.

"I won the 1988 Arkansas Invitational on Bull Shoals Lake during treacherous October fishing conditions by finessing a 4-inch, small diameter, hand-poured worm. The water along the stairstepped end of the bluff I fished dropped from 35 to 120 feet," Klein notes.

The worm was impaled on a 1/0 hook teamed with a 3/16-ounce bullet weight and 6-pound line. During a difficult week of fishing, the little worm enabled him to weigh in 18 bass (mostly smallmouth and spotted bass) that totaled 30 pounds.

Another excellent finesse lure in his tacklebox is a 3 1/2-inch curled-tailed worm, which he customarily fishes on a 1/8-ounce jighead with an exposed hook. With that light jig and 6-pound line, the lure falls fairly fast, so you can cover a lot of water during the course of the day.

"As a finesse fisherman," Klein says, "I generally prefer to use more of a horizontal 'dragging' retrieve rather than a vertical presentation. In the fall, when these little baits are at their best, the water level in reservoirs is usually dropping, so it is clear and, with shorter days, is becoming cooler.

"Bass often are suspended in this situation, and that makes it difficult to position your boat over

to develop a feel for these seemingly mismatched components."

An excellent but overlooked finesse bait is a small (1/8 ounce) spoon, which Klein has found to be deadly in clear water and after a cold front. He likes Crippled Herring and Kastmaster spoons and fishes them on a spinning rod with 6- to 8-pound-test line.

"I usually fish the little spoons by casting and retrieving; if I need to jig a spoon vertically, I usually go to a heavier, 3/4-ounce lure," he explains. "But when casting it with

them and fish vertically without spooking them.

"Consequently, I prefer to keep the lure out away from the boat. In the Bull Shoals tournament, I basically dragged the bait behind as the boat drifted. That proved to be the ultimate finesse presentation."

Using a traditional doodling or shaking technique enabled him to win another tough tournament on Georgia's Lake Lanier. In that event, he had the most success by fishing a 4-inch straight-tailed worm around deep water boat docks in clear water.

Doodling is a finesse technique that he sometimes refers to as "deep-flipping." Using a finesse worm on a 1/0 hook, 3/16-ounce slip sinker, 6-pound line and a flexible-tip 5 1/2-foot spinning rod, he quietly approaches a boathouse and makes a short pitch to its vertical pilings. While the worm is falling, he shakes the rod tip slightly to give the lure extra action. Once it reaches the bottom, he raises the worm a few inches off the bottom and shakes it several times.

An excellent tool for doodling is a 4-inch ring worm, which has great built-in action. Perhaps the most famous — and certainly one of the most productive — sissy baits is the tube jig.

"On a 1/16-ounce head, the Gitzit tube is one of the best finesse lures you'll find," says Klein. "The lure is very effective due to its size (about 1 1/2 inches in length), which is similar to that of the average baitfish. It is especially productive in clear water, but it is also an underrated bait for stained water. Its only disadvantage is that you have to fish it on light line (6-pound is best). But to the experienced angler, that isn't a major handicap."

The Gitzit is most effective when fished vertically. The key to the bait is the way it falls in a spiral, leaving a trail of little air bubbles that really seem to attract bass. The most effective way to catch fish on a tube bait is on the initial drop, especially in shallow water. In shallow cover, a Gitzit usually doesn't fall more than about 3 feet before a fish hits it.

"I fish the Gitzit deep and have a lot of success

that way. It takes a long time for that little bait to reach 30- and 40-foot depths, but once I get it down there, I drag it or let it drift with the trolling motor. That's a very effective method," he adds.

Sissy baits are a much-maligned class of lures. But finesse techniques are becoming a more important facet of bass fishing with each passing year. And in the future, even the most macho bass enthusiast will need to resort to sissy tactics if he is to stay on the cutting edge of the sport.

MAKING INACTIVE FISH strike a lure is one of the rewards of reaction baits.

TRIGGERING A REACTION BITE
Bass don't have to be hungry to strike

ASK ANY BASS FISHERMAN about reaction baits, and you'll probably get a fairly consistent account of how crankbaits, spinnerbaits, topwater plugs and jerkbaits can trigger responses from bass in neutral or negative moods. Although their answers might be correct, in most cases they would be incomplete.

(Opposite page)
EVEN WHEN FISHED slowly, a jerkbait can draw a reaction strike.

Far too often, bass fishermen view reaction baits only in "big picture" terms and never truly understand the subtleties of what constitutes a reaction bait or how and when to properly present one.

Pros like California's Skeet Reese know that reaction strikes happen when the bait is worked aggressively to trigger strikes, whether or not the fish are in a feeding mode. Some anglers make the mistake of thinking they are eliciting a reaction bite when in truth they are working the bait in a conventional fashion.

"A reaction bait is any lure that requires working the rod tip and the reel to affect the presentation," notes Reese.

"You can always find a reaction bite," he believes. "Remember, there is always more than one pattern going on any lake. There might be a group of fish on a rockpile, while another bunch is buried in cover and others are suspended on outside ledges. There is always a reaction bite — as long as you find the proper area."

THE REACTIVE BASS

Although many anglers believe that reaction baits are primarily used when bass are exhibiting a neutral or negative mood, they are actually a triggering mechanism for fish of any disposition.

Reese believes that reaction fish can be feeding fish. Far too many anglers overlook the one overriding purpose of reaction baits: to force a bass to commit, regardless of its feeding mode.

Pro Profile
SKEET REESE
Hometown: Auburn, Calif.
Birthdate: 6-30-1969

BASS Career Highlights
Tournament Titles: 2 (2003 Florida Showdown Pro, 2000 Arizona Invitational)
Times in the Classic: 3
Times in the Money: 35
Total Weight: 1,606 lbs., 14 ozs.
Career Winnings: $386,957
Avg. Per Tournament: $6,671.67

Skeet Reese has proved his skills for making passive fish bite by winning two BASS events held under extremely tough conditions.

Regardless of the "force" required in prompting any bass to strike, presentation is always the key ingredient. Specifically, placing the lure within the strike zone, giving it the proper action and keeping it there long enough for the bass to make the commitment. Moreover, the size of the strike zone varies widely with the season, prevailing conditions and the aggressive nature of the fish themselves. By paying close attention to how far a bass will move to a bait, an angler can then select a lure that (1) will stay at the proper depth for the longest amount of time and (2) can be worked most effectively in that "commitment" area. A good example of this is a jigging spoon fished in cold water, where strike zones are generally small and the lure must exhibit the most erratic action in a limited space.

The fundamental theory behind triggering a reaction strike is to make the bait mimic the predatory instinct of the bass. Erratic movement is the key, Reese emphasizes.

THE REACTION LURE

Of the various factors that govern the effectiveness of reaction baits, speed is perhaps the most important. But, since anything from soft jerkbaits to 1/2-ounce jigs can be used for reaction strikes, "speed" does not always mean "fast."

"If you throw a soft jerkbait, let it sink and twitch it once, it's still a reaction bait. It's just a reaction bait fished slowly," counsels Reese. "On the other end of the spectrum

would be something like a Speed Trap or Rat-L-Trap (lipless crankbaits) burned along as fast as you can reel."

Although reaction baits often lean toward the faster side of the equation, finding the proper speed only becomes productive when combined with the correct presentation.

Whether it's a fast, slow or moderate retrieve, the triggering mechanism in reaction baits is usually a quick movement, a fast fall or a sudden change in direction. Depending on the cover or structure being fished, a fisherman can either impart that triggering movement through his rod and reel or by ricocheting the lure off submerged cover. Whatever the case, speed and directional changes are the two components when using lures as reaction baits.

COVER AND CONDITIONS

While every fishing situation poses a slightly different set of problems, cover, structure and water clarity are three related factors that often dictate different approaches with reaction baits.

For pure reaction strikes, the presence of cover or complex structure greatly simplifies the procedure. With either visible or submerged targets, the strike zones around these areas are relatively easy to gauge, plus you're targeting bass that are not on the move.

"If you're dealing with fish around cover or structure, you're dealing with a more isolated bass. This is their home, their domain. These are the fish most likely to strike out of aggression," says Reese.

"If you bounce a spinnerbait off a brushpile and it comes right by its head, the fish really doesn't know what to do, other than grab it. The same holds true with a crankbait or jerkbait."

In this scenario, a faster retrieve preys on this heightened aggression level by raising curiosity and sparking predatory instincts. And most importantly, it all happens in an instant.

However, without the benefit of cover or structure, bass are forced to move farther to the bait, thereby greatly expanding that critical commitment zone to a point where all sorts of things can go wrong. Now, it becomes a matter of finesse — being able to

A REACTION STRIKE is an attention grabber, making lure contact with structure a key.

use a bait and presentation that gives the fish more time to reach the lure and then delivers the right moves to elicit a reaction. Too fast or too slow, too harsh or too subtle, and the jig is up — especially since bass in open water can exhibit the gamut of moods from neutral to somewhat aggressive.

If a fisherman didn't already have enough to consider, water clarity also plays a significant role in bait selection and presentation. Since bass primarily feed in one of two ways — either by sight or vibration — the right water clarity can greatly affect an angler's results.

In off-colored water, a fisherman can get away with more in terms of lure size and color. When the scene shifts to clear water, these two factors take on far greater importance.

A REACTION BITE is the only option for catching sluggish bass immediately after the spawn.

YEAR-ROUND REACTIONS

Overriding all these concerns about lures and presentations are a variety of seasonal considerations that not only dictate fish aggressiveness, but also determine their positions on cover or structure.

Prespawn — As the water starts to warm, jerkbaits and similar lures become more effective. These lures have a lot of action, but stay in the strike zone longer.

Reese figures that bass are staging for the spawn and may not be hungry, so they must be triggered into biting. "At this time of year, I want a hard, erratic action. With jerkbaits, a solid, sharp snap of the rod tip delivers an erratic darting motion that triggers a lot of those strikes. Many of these bass get hooked outside the mouth. They're coming up, looking at it and striking violently."

Spawn — Even in the prespawn period, bass start developing that territorial instinct where they are more interested in chasing the bait than trying to eat it. In this scenario, productive colors include perch and sunfish. Treble-hooked baits are also a plus. In case the fish strikes the bait, it can be hooked with the multiple barbs.

Since spawning bass are more territorial, says Reese, you need to keep the bait in the strike zone longer. If you're working the bait too quickly, you won't stay in that zone. You need a lure that offers maximum action without moving too far — a soft jerkbait, for example. "Don't worry about cover," he adds, "because they can be in the thickest tangle or along wide-open banks."

Postspawn — Bass are tired, sluggish and not back to their normal feeding routines. You have to be a little creative and try any number of things from a fast falling jig to a jerkbait dancing in front of them to a spinnerbait flashing right in front of their noses.

"For anyone who wants to catch large fish on a topwater bait, postspawn is the time to do it. Typically, you've got a lot of males guarding fry and the females have backed out," Reese has found. "These female bass are rather lethargic, but when they feed, they want something larger and something that looks easy. Although postspawn can be

an all-or-nothing proposition, if you've got the right water clarity, Zara Spooks, poppers and buzzbaits can produce some of your biggest catches of the year."

Summer — Faster speeds are more important now, during what is probably the best time for reaction bites. A wider variety of baits are productive because fish are scattered through all zones. Many times, the ultimate summertime reaction bait is a crankbait. If you can find bass relating to some type of cover or the bottom, then try to make a crankbait ricochet around, move erratically and make noise.

Reese notes that bass feed most heavily in low light periods, so reaction presentations are required at midday. "If the wind is blowing, it can produce the best reaction bites you'll ever experience. The wind breaks up light penetration and acts much like cloud cover or low light. I rely on a Horizon spinnerbait or a crankbait in a shad pattern," he notes.

Fall — During this time of the year, anglers can choose between fishing the bottom and triggering surface bites. As water temperatures cool, bass get more excited, and you'll receive more feeding bites. Even so, pay close attention to those triggering movements, whether you're throwing a jerkbait, Zara Spook or spinnerbait. Sometimes, it's that last little bit of action that gets them to strike.

Fall is crankbait time for Reese, because water temperatures are dropping and bass are schooling and feeding heavily. Bass in the lakes he fishes will either chase shad or crawfish, and lures need to look and move like those two forms of forage.

Winter — You can still trigger reaction bites in winter, but because of the colder water temperatures, the strike zone is much more limited.

"In winter, much depends on the water clarity. In clear water, you can get reaction bites on crankbaits or spinnerbaits," believes Reese. "This is especially true with spotted bass. But probably the best reaction bait will be a spoon."

REACTION presentations are required at midday since bass feed most heavily in low light periods.

CATCHING BASS YOU CAN SEE

Master the difficult art of sight fishing for bass

IT CAN BE the most exciting and frustrating fishing of all.

Sight fishing for bass, the way the guides in the Florida Keys stalk bonefish on the flats, ignites an adrenaline rush like no other type of bass fishing. Visual fishing has the same allure as topwater fishing, but with one major difference: in this game, you get to see the fish even before it strikes.

It is this visual element of clear water fishing that creates such an intimidating and frustrating experience when the fish don't cooperate. It's unsettling enough not to get bites in stained or muddy water, when you can't be sure a bass is near the lure. But it's doubly unnerving when you can see the fish and it refuses to strike.

Shaw Grigsby is one of the masters of the specialized art of catching visible bass. His skill at sight fishing for ultraspooky bass in clear water laid the foundation for his success as a BASS pro, although he is also one of the sport's most versatile anglers.

After two decades of tournament fishing, Grigsby has refined what at one time was a highly specialized technique into a mainstream application that can be used anywhere bass are found.

The common denominator for sight fishing is clear water, a condition that prevails in Florida and other stops on the pro tour.

"I like clear water bass fishing because it's a challenge," Grigsby says. "It's real exciting to see the fish ahead of time, work the bait just right to get it interested and then watch it charge the bait. To me, it's the ultimate."

Anglers who avoid clear water figure that if they can see the bass, the bass can see them, and that makes it harder to draw strikes.

But Grigsby says the lack of fishing pressure on these visible bass works to his advantage. "I will often have an area to myself, rather than having to share stained water areas with other fishermen," he says. "Some people get psyched out because they may see a lot of fish, but only catch one out of 100 if they're not real adept at this type of fishing."

Contrary to popular opinion, sight fishing is more than just bed fishing for spawning bass. That certainly is a productive time for sight fishing, but it is by no means limited to spawning season. Grigsby and several of his peers have proved that on the BASS circuit.

Grigsby seeks out clear water and visible bass in

his travels throughout the year, with the exception of the coldest times, when most bass migrate to deeper water.

As with other types of fishing, conditions dictate when sight fishing will be most productive.

The ideal conditions for chasing visible bass are a bright, overcast day — enough clouds to hide the sun, but plenty of sunlight penetration for seeing beneath the water's surface — and little or no wind. The cloud cover makes clear water bass slightly less wary, Grigsby says. The exception to his preference for cloud cover is spawning season, when bright days are best. Bass that are protecting a nest are more likely to hold in that position and less likely to spook under sunny skies.

"Spawning bass are a whole different game

Pro Profile
SHAW GRIGSBY
Hometown: Gainesville, Fla.
Birthdate: 5-11-1956

BASS Career Highlights
Tournament Titles: 8 (2000 Georgia Top 150 Pro, 2000 Florida Top 150 Pro, 1999 Florida Invitational, 1997 Georgia Top 100 Pro, 1993 Georgia Top 100 Pro Division, 1992 Texas Invitational, 1990 Texas Invitational, 1988 Texas Invitational)
Times in the Classic: 9
Times in the Money: 100
Total Weight: 5,197 lbs., 15 ozs.
Career Winnings: $1,194,655.30   **Avg. Per Tournament:** $6,354.55

Shaw Grigsby gained access to the BASS millionaire's club by chasing visible bass.

Sight Fishing Lures

Grigsby relies on tubes and lizards to do the lion's share of his sight fishing. Some BASS pros expand their arsenal. Here are some other options to consider when traditional bed baits don't work:

■ 6- and 8-inch straight-tail worms rigged weightless
■ Floater/diver minnow ("jerkbait")
■ 4-inch straight-tail worm or lizard rigged Texas style
■ 3-inch plastic crawfish rigged Texas style
■ 1/2-ounce jig-and-pig

from regular sight fishing," Grigsby explains. "Bedding fish don't want to bite, so you have to really work those fish. Generally, they're harder to catch. They're finicky because they are not feeding, they are protecting. It takes a different style of fishing to catch them."

Grigsby utilizes a variety of lures for visible bass, including minnow plugs, tube jigs, small worms, a downsized jig-and-pig, in-line spinners and noisy surface lures.

A new trick he's learned is to fish a Strike King 3X Zulu, a superbuoyant soft jerkbait.

"The whole body of this bait wiggles when you move it," he notes. "The bait is so flexible it vibrates down its whole side. And it will float with a 4/0 or 5/0 hook."

He sometimes uses a heavy hook wrapped with lead tape to make the Zulu suspend. He twitches a suspending bait. "If you put a bullet weight in front of the 3X Zulu, you can work it like a darting minnow. When you stop it, instead of it sink-

Sight Fishing For Prespawn Bass

Keep these factors in mind when fishing for prespawn bass:

1. Where there is good water clarity, bass move out of deeper wintering areas in spring to begin a migration into their spawning areas. They move in increments, holding on pieces of cover along the way as they wait for the water temperature to rise to an optimum level for spawning (mid-60s to 72 degrees). Likely target areas include boat docks, fallen trees, brushpiles and retaining walls.

2. Boat positioning is very critical when visible bass are staging on targets. These fish are very aware of what's going on around them and are in a feeding mode prior to the spawn. It's imperative to maintain a safe distance between you and the fish. Also avoid turning your trolling motor on, as it will spook the fish.
3. Begin casting a 6- or 8-inch floating worm to the bass.
4. While high visibility colors are easy to see, bass often get conditioned not to hit them. Try natural colors — green, brown, black, etc.
5. Hitting a precise target is not as critical now as it will be when the bass are bedding. The fish will move off the cover to strike. Make random casts around the target until you contact bass.

ing down to the bottom like other soft jerkbaits, it floats back to the top. This bait suspends like a lifelike shad that has stopped in motion."

Critical in sight fishing is to use a lure you can see easily. You need to be able to watch the bait as you're working it and when a strike occurs.

Catching visible bass demands using light tackle and thin line. Grigsby uses a 6-foot medium action rod and a wide spool spinning reel loaded with 6- to 10-pound-test monofilament line.

One of the most important pieces of equipment for sight fishing, Grigsby says, is a pair of quality sunglasses with good polarization and with ultraviolet protection. Glasses come in gray, amber or yellow glass lenses for varying light conditions.

Perhaps most crucial to stalking visible bass is the initial approach. Unlike a camouflaged hunter in the woods, an approaching angler has a good chance of being seen by clear water bass.

"You have to present a bait to the fish before it can see you, because once it sees you, it gets real tough to catch," Grigsby says.

Obviously, you should avoid brightly colored clothing. But boat positioning is even more important. Sight fishing requires positioning the boat at an angle that permits seeing and casting to the bass, without being detected easily by the fish.

By following those procedures, Grigsby usually is able to entice a bass to strike. Put another way, what he sees — most of the time — is what he gets.

Sight Fishing For Prespawn "Cruisers"

"Cruisers" are prespawn bass that aren't holding to targets. Instead, these fish can be spotted swimming near the surface or along shallow weedlines or objects. Keep these facts in mind when sight fishing for cruising bass:

1. Cruisers are tough to catch. They aren't focused on eating, but rather are driven by instinct to find the right nesting spot. While they are tempting to fish for, they can be very time consuming to catch — an important consideration if you're fishing a tournament.

2. The best way to catch a cruiser is to lead the fish by a long distance with a small lure fished on the bottom, such as a tube bait or baby craw. Determine the direction in which the fish is moving and cast 15 to 25 feet past the fish.

3. Move the bait with extreme subtlety. Many pros report their best success comes by not moving the bait at all until the bass swims over to investigate it. If you see the bass inhale the bait, drop the rod tip and set the hook hard.

4. If a cruising bass doesn't make a move for a dark colored lure in two or three attempts, try a light colored worm, or vice versa.

5. As an alternative to a small sinking lure, a small, silver, hard jerkbait twitched gently on top may draw a strike from a cruiser.

PATTERNS

An intimate knowledge
of bass behavior makes success
commonplace . . .

THE FOUR SEASONS OF BASS

Finding the pattern begins with the season

PROFESSIONAL BASS ANGLERS are adept at finding and catching bass under all conditions. Part of their expertise comes from knowing where bass live during the four seasons, and how they move as one season shifts to another.

Veteran Oklahoma BASS pro and former fisheries biologist Ken Cook has an in-depth knowledge of where largemouth, smallmouth and spotted bass locate from one season to the next.

His insight about seasonal behavior is explained in layman terms in the following summary.

GENERAL FACTS ABOUT BASS LOCATION

Bass are coldblooded creatures, meaning that their body temperature is directly related to the temperature of the water in which they swim. Thus the temperature of the water can have a great deal of impact on where bass will be and how active they are on any given day.

In general, bass in most lakes and reservoirs are most active when the water ranges from approximately 60 to 85 degrees. Bass will be less active in colder or warmer water. In cold weather, bass will usually seek out the warmest water they can find, provided they don't have to move too far to find it.

The amount of cover (weeds, rocks, submerged wood, etc.) that exists in the water varies dramatically from one lake to the next. Some lakes are full of weeds; others have acres of standing timber. Still others appear barren, with little visible cover at all. The amount, location and type of cover available to the bass also will help determine its location at any given time during the year. Cover is not as important to smallmouth bass as it is to largemouth, and is important to spotted bass only at certain times of the year.

Perhaps most important, the bass is driven to new locations throughout the four seasons by its need for food and procreation. Bass will move into certain areas for spawning. Other areas might better serve their forage needs.

Bass do not "migrate" in the same sense that waterfowl do. An individual bass doesn't usually move a great distance during the course of the year; rather, bass try to locate in areas where all of their seasonal needs can be met without traveling long distances.

Some species of bass inhabit different depth zones than others. Largemouth bass, in most bodies of water, are shallow water creatures much of the year. Smallmouth bass spend most of their time deeper than largemouth. Spotted bass have

been tracked at depths to 100 feet, but will also inhabit shallow water during the course of the year.

LARGEMOUTH LOCATIONS

Winter — In most bodies of water, the largemouth bass will locate near the deepest parts of the lake, but usually not in extremely deep water. Many bass will navigate to the main lake and hold around bluffs, channel ledges and channel banks, and the ends and sides of deeper points. Food is not a tremendous factor driving largemouth bass location during the winter months, since bass consume far less forage in cold water than in warm water, and digestion takes much longer as well.

Finding the warmest possible water can be a major key to largemouth location now. "If you can

Pro Profile
KEN COOK
Hometown: Meers, Okla.
Birthdate: 2-2-1947

BASS Career Highlights
Tournament Titles: 6 (1991 CITGO Bassmaster Classic, 1987 New York Invitational, 1983 Missouri Invitational, 1983 Super Bass Tournament, 1982 Florida Invitational, 1980 Chapter Championship)
Times in the Classic: 14
Times in the Money: 120
Total Weight: 5,529 lbs., 5 ozs.
Career Winnings: $640,067.20
Avg. Per Tournament: $2,723.69

As a former fishery biologist, Ken Cook's inside knowledge of bass behavior gives him a competitive edge on the BASS tour.

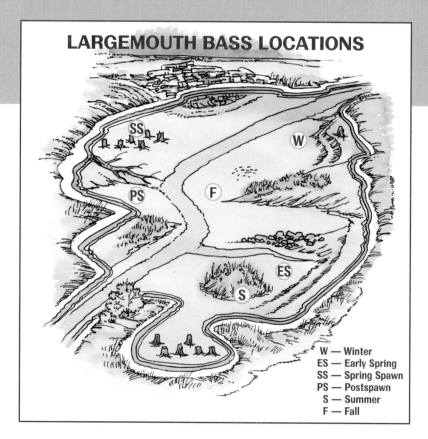

LARGEMOUTH BASS LOCATIONS

W — Winter
ES — Early Spring
SS — Spring Spawn
PS — Postspawn
S — Summer
F — Fall

CREEK CHANNELS like the one in this illustration provide a seasonal travel corridor for bass.

WHEN LARGEMOUTH suspend and school during the summertime, an electronic graph is the best means of tracking their movements.

find some water that's a few degrees warmer than elsewhere in the system, and that water is of good quality, you can sometimes load the boat in winter," says Cook.

Early spring — The slowly rising temperature of the water and the lengthening daylight period are cues to largemouth bass that they should begin moving shallower. "Look for ditches, channel banks, stumpfields, fencerows and other structures leading from deep to shallower water in the prespawn period; these serve as pathways along which bass make a move to their spring locations," Cook notes.

Largemouth bass seldom stay in shallow water for extended lengths of time in early spring; rather, they hold where deep and shallow water meet and make short feeding forays into shallower areas. "Breaklines are critical structures during the prespawn period; here largemouth have access to both deep

and shallow water only a few feet apart," Cook notes. "By locating over a breakline, say a dropoff at the end of a big flat that drops from 25 to 8 feet, bass can hold in deep water when they are less active, and they can travel up into the shallows to feed. Determining the timing of these short, infrequent feeding movements is critical to fishing success. Check them several times throughout the course of the day."

Spring spawn — Largemouth bass prefer to spawn in shallow water. They often bed in coves and tributaries protected from the chilling effects of a harsh north wind. The nest will usually be no deeper than the depth at which sunlight can penetrate to incubate the eggs; according to Cook, this is seldom deeper than 4 feet.

Bass like a hard-bottom condition for spawning, as opposed to mud or silt. But these fish are highly adaptable — they have been known to spawn on the tops of submerged stumps and in old tires.

Postspawn — After spawning, many largemouth bass reverse their movements along ditches, channel banks and other "migration routes" and move back out to deeper channel structures. However, if there is sufficient cover in shallow water, they might not move far. Some

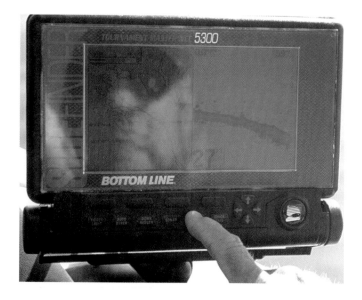

SMALLMOUTH RELATE to deeper water more so than largemouth. As a result, smallmouth will remain in deep water to spawn while largemouth move into the shallows.

might stay quite close to their spawning grounds for extended periods.

Summer — "Convex structure — humps, rockpiles, saddles and the like — is a major key to largemouth location in summer," Cook believes. "Bass will locate on these structures, and they will tend to move shallower or deeper on them as their mood dictates." Many largemouth will move into shallower water at night to feed, he adds.

In reservoirs without much current movement, stratification occurs in hot weather. Lower layers of the lake can be low in dissolved oxygen. Any flow, however insignificant, can increase dissolved oxygen levels and stack up largemouth bass; check for schools to be holding around channel dropoffs and ledges.

Fall — Largemouth tend to follow their forage more in the fall than in other months, which can make them hard to locate. Rather than relating to structural breaklines or objects, they might be out in open water, chasing big schools of shad. "Largemouth bass binge-feed in the fall," Cook has found.

"Food is plentiful and they take advantage of the best feeding opportunities. Often small, scattered groupings of bass suspend offshore or hold at the ends of long main lake points waiting for the right opportunity to 'bust' a big school of baitfish. These feeding binges often occur two or three times a day at scattered intervals."

SMALLMOUTH BASS LOCATIONS

Winter — Look for smallmouth on steep main lake banks composed of rock or gravel, as well as on the sides and ends of deep points in both the main portion of the lake and the first third of the deeper tributaries. Smallmouth also will suspend off main lake bluffs at a comfortable depth level, often 15 to 25 feet.

Prespawn — The biggest females are generally the first to begin "staging" or moving into shallower areas in preparation for spawning. As the water warms to approximately 56 degrees, look for big smallmouth on the deep edges of main lake gravel

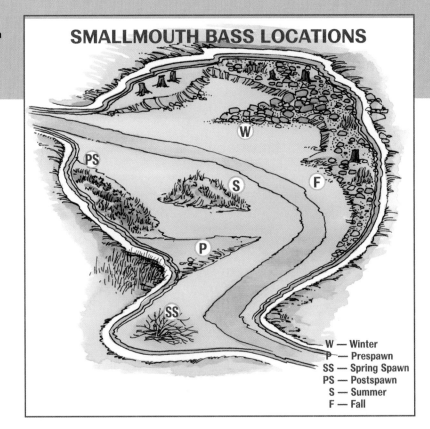

SMALLMOUTH BASS LOCATIONS

W — Winter
P — Prespawn
SS — Spring Spawn
PS — Postspawn
S — Summer
F — Fall

USE SPIDER JIGS to catch bronzebacks suspended along main lake bluffs adjacent to tapering pea gravel shorelines.

flats, or on the tips of long, slow-tapering clay points. These fish will stay in the 15- to 20-foot zone much of the day but will move up shallower to feed, usually not much shallower than 6 feet.

Spring spawn — Smallmouth tend to spawn in deeper water than do largemouth, down to 12 feet or more in some clear reservoirs, but more often 6 to 8 feet. Look for spawners on main lake gravel flats, especially those with a sparse peppering of stumps or scattered clumps of thin weeds. Some smallmouth also will spawn at the ends of slow-tapering points as well as on the tops of humps, provided these are shallow enough.

Postspawn — Some smallmouth will hang around flooded bushes close to their spawning beds for a few days; others will gravitate to the ends of spawning flats and suspend out over deep water, often 15 to 30 feet down. These fish will make occasional shallower movements to chase schools of baitfish; surface feeding is common now.

Summer — In reservoirs lacking current, smallmouth often suspend over river or creek channels and station themselves 20 to 50 feet deep. In large lakes, such as Lake Erie, they might suspend in mas-

IN RESERVOIRS that have soft bottoms, look for bass to spawn on chunk rock or gravel laden banks.

sive numbers over deep reefs, rockpiles and other midlake structures. Where weedbeds are present, smallies are likely to be considerably shallower, but they are not as prone to hide inside dense weedbeds as are largemouth. Instead, look for them on the outer edges and tops of the beds. Nighttime feeding movements are common in summer; these fish often move shallow on points and 45 degree rock banks to feed on crawfish after dark. In reservoirs with current, main lake rockpiles and humps hold many fish during periods of intense generation during the day. At night, they'll be extremely shallow on main lake bars and stumpflats subject to strong current flow.

Fall — Some smallmouth bass will gather on main lake points, where they will chase schools of baitfish. Others will gravitate to 45 degree rock banks and stay very deep — 50 feet isn't uncommon in highland lakes — until the lake turns over.

SPOTTED BASS LOCATIONS

SPOTTED BASS LOCATIONS

W — Winter
SS — Spring Spawn
S — Summer
F — Fall

SPOTTED BASS LOCATIONS

Winter — Great numbers of spotted bass sometimes suspend around standing submerged trees in deep, clear reservoirs; these fish might hold 30 feet deep in more than 100 feet of water. Other groupings of spots can be found in V-shaped coves or "hollows," where they suspend in numbers around baitfish schools.

Spring — Spotted bass move shallower to spawn via channels and channel banks leading to main lake flats and tributaries. Areas with pea gravel are especially preferred for spawning. Bedding takes place in water just slightly cooler than that which largemouth bass prefer for spawning, but warmer than smallmouth like. After the spawn, spotted bass gorge themselves on shad and other baitfish. Brushy areas in creek arms hold schools of baitfish; spotted bass often are drawn to these in the postspawn, but are not as likely to be deep within the brushpiles as largemouth might be, preferring instead to prowl the open water outside the cover.

Summer — Spotted bass are prone to suspend in deep water on main lake structure, often above the thermocline and usually near a school of baitfish. They often feed at night in hot weather, moving shallower via long, tapering main lake sand or mud points or midlake rockpiles.

Fall — Scattered schools, each consisting of large numbers of spots, will roam open water, gorging on shad at various intervals throughout the day. Schooling often occurs off main lake points and over offshore structures — such as humps, rockpiles or river channel ledges.

WHEN COMPARED with other species, spotted bass are more likely to suspend over offshore structure in deeper water.

SPRING THROUGH FALL, it's hard to beat a spinnerbait as a search tool. Fish it on banks, near wood, over submerged structure and off deep ledges. Once you get bit, refine your bait choice to the situation.

FINDING THE ACTIVITY ZONE: WHERE BASS BITE

Before wetting a lure, determine the best depth

W HEN THE PROS are trying to establish patterns that will carry them through three or four days of tournament competition, they often begin their search by looking for an "activity zone" — the basic depth in which both baitfish and bass seem to be located. Once this activity zone is determined, appropriate lure choices and fine-tuning of the pattern can begin.

"Finding the activity zone basically involves figuring out how deep the bass are," explains veteran BASS pro Alton Jones. "It is more critical in summer and winter, when bass tend to be in deeper water. But it's an important part of pattern fishing anytime, because it can be influenced by water temperature, current, forage or other changing conditions."

Activity zones can be in shallow water, and this is where many pros, including Jones, begin their search. Using spinnerbaits, crankbaits, tubes and jigs, they explore different shallow water options, such as boat docks, visible cover, grassbeds or rocky shorelines.

"While I'm fishing these types of places, I look for any clues that might tell me where the bass are — herons feeding along the bank or bass chasing baitfish," he says. "The clues tell me the activity zone is in shallow water, and that can be very important, especially if I'm not catching fish."

When you do catch fish and determine the activity zone is shallow, all may be well and good, but sometimes when you return to those fish, you discover the unthinkable: They're gone.

"This happens more often than we like to think about," says Jones. "Simple factors like fishing pressure and boat traffic can cause bass to move 4 or 5 feet deeper. When I experience something like this, the first thing I do is move straight out to the nearest deeper water, such as farther out on a sloping bank or point, or perhaps to the edge of the first breakline. I'm fishing the same general area, but at a greater depth.

"This is really the solution you hope to find, because it's the easiest to adjust to," he continues. "I'll change to a heavier spinnerbait or a deeper diving crankbait and keep right on fishing. Generally, moving from shallow to deeper water is the sequence I follow in spring and fall, when bass are most likely to be shallow."

THE "ACTIVITY ZONE" refers to the depth where both bass and baitfish are found in the water column.

In the summer and also in winter, when bass are likely to be deeper, Jones relies more on his electronics to find an activity zone. In those seasons, baitfish gather in huge schools and show up clearly on sonar. Bass often position themselves just below the baitfish.

"I go out on the main body of the lake and turn on my depthfinder," Jones explains. "I idle back and forth across deeper channels, points and flats. Soon, I begin to notice very distinctly that baitfish are holding within a certain range, such as 15 to 18 feet, or 22 to 30 feet.

"I'll see very little life above or below this range, so I know that this is the activity zone. One factor that will also help you identify this zone is knowing ahead of time what the basic depth preference

Pro Profile
ALTON JONES
Hometown: Waco, Texas
Birthdate: 7-13-1963

BASS Career Highlights
Tournament Titles: 3 (2003 California Showdown Pro, 2000 MegaBucks Pro, 1997 Alabama Top 100 Pro)
Times in the Classic: 7
Times in the Money: 46
Total Weight: 2,619 lbs., 7 ozs.
Career Winnings: $616,116.70
Avg. Per Tournament: $6,696.90

The ability to adapt to most any bass fishing situation has enabled Alton Jones to become one of the sport's most versatile anglers after more than a decade on the BASS tour.

TO FIND THE activity zone in summer, Alton Jones looks for bass holding on the end of a point — where they will suspend over a flat or hump adjacent to deep water.

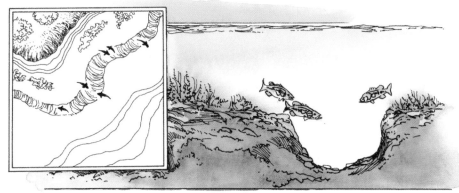

IN THE WINTER, Jones will follow a creek channel ledge corresponding with the activity zone depth. Creeks meandering through flats are prime areas.

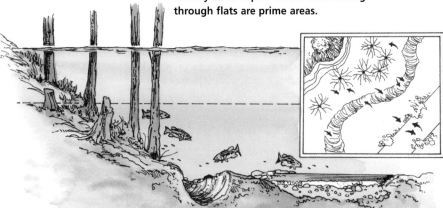

FOLLOWING POTENTIAL migration routes and probing shallow and then deep water is another method for finding the activity zone. Once the depth is established, fish textbook bass structure — such as treelines or channel ledges.

for bass is at that time of year. Bass on every lake have a seasonal depth preference, and the better guides and fishermen on that lake will be able to tell you what it is."

In addition to the season, depth and current are important factors.

"In clear water, bass will simply be deeper," says Jones. "We regularly see this on many of the Western and Northern lakes, which can be much clearer than most Southern lakes.

"Current, for the most part, seems to move bass shallow. In fact, when power generation starts and current is created, bass will often move toward the shallows. The activity zone depth can actually change once or twice during a day."

Once you learn the depth of the activity zone, you have several options. One is to get a lure (a spoon, jig or deep diving crankbait) down to the fish you've just found and determine whether they'll hit. If they do hit, consider yourself fortunate, because bass suspended in open water often are inactive.

"I like to find structure that intersects with the activity zone depth," says Jones. "For example, if I consistently find schools of baitfish suspended between 22 and 25 feet, then I'll try to locate points, flats or some other feature on the bottom at that same depth."

In summer, Jones prefers to look for points along the edges of flats at this depth. Frequently, bass will locate on the tops of these points very close to where they drop into much deeper water.

In winter, he prefers to find a creek channel ledge at the right depth. He

especially likes creeks that meander through flats; he'll fish the edges, realizing bass like to locate close to steeper breaklines.

Another way to locate bass once an activity zone has been established, is to follow a possible "migration route" from shallow water out to deeper water until the depth corresponds with the activity zone. Primary migration routes include underwater roadbeds, treelines and small creek channels.

"I believe bass use features like these to keep themselves oriented," says Jones, "and anywhere you happen to find two different features at the activity zone depth, you're likely to have a bonanza. This might be where a treeline meets a roadbed, or sometimes where a roadbed crosses a creek.

"Once you do find a spot like this, mark it carefully, because bass will use it year after year.

"Finding the activity zone is probably the most overlooked part of bass pattern fishing," says Jones. "Anglers have a lot of different ways to locate bass, but many of them don't consider depth until after they're catching bass.

"I think finding the depth first is much easier. Then, when you match that depth with structure, you're nearly always very close to the fish."

AFTER LOCATING evidence of baitfish and bass, Jones uses a crankbait to reach an activity zone where bass suspend over deep structure.

JONES BEGINS his search for activity in shallow water before moving deep.

SUPER SPRING TACTICS
In spring, water temperature means everything

FOR MOST PEOPLE, there are four seasons in a year. For bass fishermen, there are six. When it comes to deciphering the seasonal patterns of bass, no knowledgeable angler would dare approach spring as one season. In terms of bass behavior and movement, there are three seasons: prespawn, spawn and postspawn. Each of these stages has a ritualistic impact on the species' habits and habitats.

When it comes to locating bass in the spring, it is critical to understand their annual migration to and from their spawning grounds, as well as the places where they undertake their vital nesting routine.

Spring is the favorite time of year for most people because bass are easier to locate then — as long as they understand the importance of water temperature. In fact, experienced pros across the country rely on water temperature to help them navigate through the changes of the miniseasons from prespawn to bedding time to postspawn.

"Water temperature tells the bass what to do and when to move. And it can do the same for you," emphasizes Arizona pro Dean Rojas, whose

record setting spawning-time catch of five bass weighing 45 pounds, 2 ounces, is already legendary.

Some anglers prefer fishing for prespawn bass, while others are die-hard bed fishermen. Rojas points out that using a temperature gauge can enable you to exploit your favorite stage of spring longer by pinpointing a certain temperature range around the lake or reservoir.

"The key is understanding the heating cycle of the lake — knowing which areas heat up earliest and latest, and then following that ideal temperature around the lake," Rojas says.

PRESPAWN

If you could survey most experienced bass anglers regarding their absolute favorite times to fish,

Pro Profile
DEAN ROJAS
Hometown: Grand Saline, Texas
Birthdate: 7-31-1971

BASS Career Highlights
Tournament Titles: 2 (2001 Louisiana Top 150 Pro, 2001 Florida Top 150 Pro)
Times in the Classic: 2
Times in the Money: 29
Total Weight: 1,457 lbs., 3 ozs.
Career Winnings: $429,491
Avg. Per Tournament: $7,534.93

Dean Rojas caught 108 pounds, 12 ounces of spawning bass in four days to set the all-time heaviest winning weight in modern BASS competition.

most would select the prespawn phase. It is a time when big female bass congregate in fairly obvious places and feed heavily as they await nature's signal to move in shallower for the spawn. They are often referred to as "staging fish."

When they're staging, bass travel from their deep winter haunts toward their spawning grounds. They'll move to a spot along the way where they find the right combination of depth, cover and, of course, food. They bunch up on points, grasslines, ledges and drops while they wait for the right temperature for spawning.

The first prespawners usually appear when the temperature is in the mid-50s. They become most active as the water approaches the 60 degree mark.

To take advantage of the earliest prespawners, Rojas advises looking for the warmest water available in the early spring. There can be as much as a 10 degree variance in water temperature, depending on the location of certain coves, shorelines and pockets. During that period, most of the lake will have a temperature in the 50s, but a few areas will be closer to 60. Those warmer zones will be magnets for prespawn bass.

Typical prespawn depths are in the 5- to 15-foot range. Look in those depths for grass patches, brushpiles, stump-laden ledges, humps, holes, submerged treetops, ditches, roadbeds,

channel bends and junctions, and other structure and cover in that depth range. Access to deep water is mandatory.

The experts agree that most of the stopping points used by prespawn bass are located 100 to 500 yards from spawning flats and coves.

Experienced anglers have learned that bass will utilize the same prespawn staging areas year after year, without fail. And they will usually be biting.

THE SPAWN

If the weather remains stable, something magical happens as the water temperature tops 60 degrees: big, heavy female bass make their final migratory push out of prespawn areas and onto bedding grounds. It's spawning time.

That final migration is something to behold. Dean Rojas would attest to that.

After a mediocre practice period for a Bassmaster Top 150 on Florida's Lake Toho, Rojas noticed the sudden appearance of giant female bass on bare spots in shallow grassbeds that had been vacant earlier that day.

"I could not believe what I saw," Rojas recalls. "I saw 10-pounders, 9-pounders, 8-pounders everywhere. I figured I had found the *honey hole*."

On that day, Rojas set the BASS record for a five bass limit with 45 pounds, 2 ounces. The previous daily catch record of 34-7 was broken four times, by Rojas and others. In the course of four days, the Arizona pro weighed in 20 bass for a whopping total of 108-12. And an estimated 21 bass weighing more than 10 pounds were caught that week.

A key to Rojas' taking advantage of that remarkable spawning action was that he had pinpointed several probable nesting areas and checked them frequently throughout the practice period as the temperature rose.

"It's important to recognize what makes a good spawning area," he says. "The top two elements would be a hard bottom and exposure to sunlight. Then, I would say protection from the wind, and decent water clarity, if available."

Typical spawning areas include shallow main lake bays, flats and pockets (as well as similar features in creeks) that offer some protection from the wind.

On most lakes, the bass population will move into these spawning areas in waves, a routine that stretches over a two to three month period. And that period offers perhaps the best chance to catch the bass of a lifetime.

POSTSPAWN

It is important to note that on large lakes and reservoirs, you can prolong your enjoyment of a certain phase of spring by moving around to find areas with the water temperature that best corresponds with your preferred stage. One pro might be hunting the warmest water, where he might find bedding bass, while a fellow competitor is searching for prespawn in colder water.

As the temperature climbs toward 70 degrees, the spawning activity will wane, and the postspawn period emerges.

For Rojas, the telltale sign that postspawn has begun is the sight of the smaller male bass guarding wads of fry that have just hatched.

As soon as the eggs are hatched, the females move around on the flats, hunting and eating, and then they back off into their prespawn spots, where they will rest for a while before moving on out to wherever they intend to live for the summer.

The pre- and postspawn stopping points for the females can be exactly the same. They might travel in slightly deeper water, and they might be suspended off the bottom, but they'll follow the same routes.

While prespawn fish seem constantly on the prowl for food, postspawn bass seem tired and slow moving. They'll eat, but they don't work hard or travel far to find food. That means fishing slower, usually with a lighter weight, and being more methodical in your presentations.

Postspawn fishing doesn't match the action associated with prespawn. Postspawn females don't seem to congregate in tight groups the way prespawn bass do, so it becomes more of a game of picking off single bass here and there.

But that, too, is one of the peculiarities associated with springtime fishing. After all, for bass enthusiasts, the calendar shows six seasons, not just four.

FOLLOWING A front, which can slow the migration of the fish, probe structure along prespawn migration routes with a soft plastic lure.

DIVIDE THE WARM season into early summer, mid-summer and late summer to simplify the process of locating summertime bass.

BEATING THE SUMMER DOLDRUMS
Sweating it out on the hottest days of the year

THERE'S NO TOUGHER TIME to catch bass consistently than summer, especially during the midday hours. By the time July rolls around, most bass anglers call it quits after just half a day. Or they fish mornings and late afternoons only.

Tournament bass pros don't have the luxury, however. The most successful competitors are those who are most consistent. They have to be sharper, work harder and sometimes invent new ways to put fish in the boat during the toughest times.

Aaron Martens, a former West Coast pro now living in the South, grew up in Southern California, where he became acclimated at a young age to fishing in the hottest time of the year. And although he has proved himself capable of winning on any lake, at any time of year, Martens says he finds summer the most challenging. He attributes much of his success during other times of the year to the patience he acquired while learning to master the summer doldrums.

USING THE SUN

So what makes summertime bassing so grueling? The truth is, bass still have to eat in the summer; in fact, they eat more in the summer than they do at any other time of year. However, they are simply more aggressive in the morning and late afternoon, and do most of their "chasing" when the water is cooler and the low light conditions allow them to feed on baitfish in open water.

This doesn't indicate that bass quit eating at midday — it just means that they switch to an "ambush"

(Opposite page)
IN SUMMER, bass can be caught shallow and deep. Focus on habitat offering shade from the summer heat when fishing in shallow water.

Pro Profile
AARON MARTENS
Hometown: Castaic, Calif.
Birthdate: 8-24-1972

BASS Career Highlights
Tournament Titles: 3 (2002 California Western Open, 2000 California Invitational, 1999 California Invitational)
Times in the Classic: 4
Times in the Money: 33
Total Weight: 1,445 lbs., 8 ozs.
Career Winnings: $352,472.34
Avg. Per Tournament: $6,650.42

Growing up in Southern California left Aaron Martens no other choice than to develop his bass fishing skills during the summer doldrums. He is always a threat to win BASS events held during hot weather.

The Heat Is On . . .
So Is The Bite

"There are always fish shallow" is a bass fishing adage that can sometimes ring hollow, especially if you've just spent eight hours following this advice, without any success. But take heart. It can be done. And the man who continually proves the point in resounding fashion is two time CITGO Bassmaster Classic presented by Busch champion George Cochran.

In winning his most recent Classic championship on Alabama's Lay Lake in 1996, Cochran refused to give in to the prevailing logic that his shallow fish could not be caught, and spent the entire tournament on a 2- to 3-foot-deep, stump-filled flat.

"I prefer fishing in shallow water because I like to pick targets apart. This way, I feel like I'm throwing my bait around fish all the time. Often, when a guy is fishing deeper water, it takes a lot of time to position the boat, and he might miss the fish by 100 yards," says Cochran.

"You can fish for hours (in deep water) and not get a bite unless you're in the right spot. In shallow water, you can see activity. You can see baitfish moving. At times, you can even see fish breaking. It just seems that the odds are in my favor by covering a lot of shallow water."

Cochran admits that constant water movement that infused oxygenated water into the shallows aided his victory at Lay Lake, but he insists that even on lakes with little current, the shallows still hold bass.

Following are some of Cochran's recommendations for superhot bassing:

GEORGE COCHRAN proved his shallow water prowess with a second place finish at the 1998 Classic where he worked crankbaits around laydown timber in water less than 3 feet deep.

■ **Head upriver** — On lakes where hot weather and the tendency of fish to hold around offshore structure makes the shallow bite even tougher, Cochran simply looks for the right kind of shallow water. To him, the upriver portion of any lake becomes his primary focus — particularly in those areas where shallow and deep water are in relatively close proximity. "When there's hot weather, not much current and a tough bite, I'm fishing up the river. I'm in dingy, off-colored water and targeting things like stumps and logs on the main river, but next to deep water. The fish I'm after are up and feeding around shallow cover."

■ **Persistence pays** — Having found this type of water, the most important attribute for any angler is persistence. In many instances, these shallow bass are only active for very brief periods of time. When the activity level drops into the dead zone, Cochran frequently makes 15 to 20 casts to the very same stump, laydown or stickup.

■ **Lures and conditions** — A fisherman must be adept at evaluating the conditions, and matching them with his lure selection. Cloud cover and wind usually make spinnerbaits, buzzbaits and other topwater lures more effective. On calm, clear days, go to worms or crankbaits. In clear water, crankbaits draw reaction strikes.

■ **Go big** — When it comes to plastic worms, one of the biggest mistakes made by fishermen is overlooking really large worms — 8-, 9- and even 11-inch versions. While the temptation may be to downsize in tough conditions, the opposite response is the correct one in hot water.

mode. When the water heats up and skies are bright, bass save energy by using the shade of structure or vegetation and pounce rather than chase. In other words, bass don't expend more energy than a meal is worth.

Rather than thinking of the sun as a hindrance, Martens uses it to his favor, taking full advantage of the fact that shade positions fish. The key to his summertime success is his ability to catch fish all day long, regardless of the position of the sun.

He starts out with topwater baits during low light conditions, targeting the more active fish, then gradually works his way down to deeper water during midday, where he fishes for the more structure-oriented fish that are positioned by the shade.

TOPWATER TIME

Although you're likely to find more bass in deeper water this time of year, the fish you catch in shallow water are usually of better quality. When fishing over shallow grass flats, main lake points or along the edge of a weedline, Martens prefers a walking stickbait, which he fishes on 12- to 15-pound-test line. And when he fishes places that don't permit the use of treble hooks — sparse tules, thicker weeds and areas with plenty of brush and stickups — he switches to a buzzbait fished on 20- to 25-pound test.

"Both will work all day long if the fish are there," Martens asserts. "Bass are just more active in the early morning and late afternoon. In calmer, tougher conditions, I throw a popper. That's my go-to bait when the water is really hot and there's not a ripple on it. I just twitch it and let it sit."

SOFT JERKBAITS

Martens always has a soft jerkbait tied on a stout rod with heavy line for fishing thick weeds, pockets and overhangs. "The jerkbait works great in the middle of the day. I pull the bait over the

tops of weeds, then let it drop down into the openings," Martens explains. "The bites are usually subtle; you have to watch your line for movement."

The lure is easy to pitch and has a quiet presentation. And because it's extremely light, he can work it slowly as it sinks. Martens uses a heavy wire hook, which serves as a keel to make the bait track better. "The bait doesn't roll on its side; it sits straight up and down. These baits attract big fish," he explains, "and small hooks often bend out."

FLIPPING SHADY POCKETS

"In summer, topwater fish are roaming and feeding because of the low light, but once the sun comes up, the shade concentrates the fish," Martens explains. "Once that happens, I target shade and objects that create shade. Worms and jigs are effective when flipped into small shady spots like overhangs. Flip the bait right into the tree and let it sink."

AARON MARTENS uses a buzzbait in sparse tules and thick weeds to catch active bass in shallow water.

A slow falling bait is essential for flipping in summer. When the bite is tough, Martens' go-to bait is a small Zipper Worm, a somewhat flat, ribbed worm. It's a slow falling bait with a big silhouette, so fish can see it falling from a good distance. Martens fishes it on 15-pound test with a 3/16-ounce bullet weight; he switches to 1/8 ounce when conditions are calm and the bite is tough. When bass are more active, he ties on a 3/8-ounce jig with a twin-tail trailer.

CRANKIN' MUDLINES

Although topwater baits can be effective throughout the day on the cool side of the lake, Martens prefers the warmer side — usually the downwind

A SOFT JERKBAIT is Aaron Martens' choice for fishing thick weeds, pockets and overhangs during midday.

Dressing For Summer

side — where the water is better oxygenated. The wind serves to turn the surface layers, providing more nutrients for the fish. Mudlines are created, and they're an excellent source of quality fish during the summer.

"Most of the dirt is on the surface, which creates a warm top layer, and the water beneath the mudline is clear and cool," Martens explains. "The shade makes bass feel relaxed enough to move about, so they're generally more active."

Mudlines ordinarily range between 1 inch and 3 feet, and they act as a natural form of shade, like cloud cover, which puts bass in a more aggressive mood. Texas or Carolina rigged worms are very effective when fished beneath mudlines, but crankbaits work even better. Martens likes diving baits that run 8 to 15 feet deep.

DEEP PATTERNS

Some bass always remain deep in summer. In July and August, bass occasionally move as deep as 50 to 60 feet on the lakes Martens fishes. Most of the bass, however, are in 15 to 20 feet off structure breaks, such as flats that drop off on one side; or little humps or submerged islands. Creek channels always hold fish, but in summer, Martens focuses most of his attention on the outside structure.

Whether he's dragging a Carolina rig or shaking a Texas rig, Martens always works his bait downhill when fishing deep in the summer. He positions the boat away from where the fish are holding, then he faces into the wind and casts on top of the break. He fishes the downwind side of the break, working his bait downhill. The fish are either on top of the break or

DURING summertime, fish the downwind side of a lake where the water is high in oxygen. The wind concentrates the food supply for the fish and creates a shady mudline used by the fish to ambush prey.

WEAR BRIGHT, longsleeve shirts in summertime and periodically apply sunscreen to exposed skin areas to prevent sunburn.

on the side of it, he says. One spot can be as good as the other.

SHAKIN' WORMS

Martens' favorite method for fishing deep is "shakin' " a 6- or 7-inch Texas rigged worm, using 8- to 12-pound line (depending on water clarity) and a 3/16- or 1/4-ounce bullet weight, which he pegs.

"As a guideline, I use brighter colors for brighter days and darker colors for darker days," he reveals. "I prefer more transparent shades for clearer water; solid shades like black-grape for darker, stained water. In extremely clear water, a transparent worm with flake gets bit better than something without flake." He determines the flake color by finding out the color of worm that bass usually bite on the lake he's fishing. That is, if bass prefer blue worms on a certain lake, he uses transparent worms with blue flake.

CAROLINA RIGGING

Carolina rigs can cover a lot of water in short order. "The large weight makes noise as it churns up the bottom, and bass move in to investigate, expecting to find a crawfish," Martens asserts. "For that reason, when I'm Carolina rigging, I tend to stick to crawfish colors, like watermelon, pumpkinseed and grape. The best baits I've found for Carolina rigging are lizards and Zipper worms. I use 15-pound test as my main line and 10- to 12-pound for the leader."

SPLIT SHOTTING: THE LAST RESORT

When the bite is really tough, and he's just looking for one or two keepers to fill out his limit, Martens split shots a 4-inch worm on 6-pound line. Because a split shot is much smaller than the weight used on a Carolina rig, the bass' attention stays focused on the bait, not the sinker. When split shotting, Martens uses lighter, shadlike colors, such as smoke/sparkle and blue neon, because when the bait is suspended off the bottom, the bass are looking for a shad, minnow, sculpin or some other baitfish.

"If I had to pick a favorite time of year to fish, it would be summer," says Martens. "It's more challenging when conditions are tough. In the summer, you have to work to put fish in the boat.

"Most people prefer to fish only during the good times. That's too bad, because the best way to improve your skills is to fish when conditions are toughest. That's what hones your skills, makes you think more and helps you develop new skills that you can use when conditions are difficult — any time of year."

SHALLOW and deep patterns in summertime open up the tacklebox. For a versatile angler, it can be a godsend.

USE LIPLESS CRANKBAITS in the fall when bass are feeding on shad.

FAIL-SAFE FALL PATTERNS
Don't pass up these hot spots in autumn

IF BASS FISHING has a coronation period, it is the fall of the year.

Spring, with its fat and accessible spawning bass, is a great time to fish. Summer can provide some excellent "numbers" action on some lakes and reservoirs. And there are times in winter when bass will congregate heavily on certain deep water hot spots.

But nothing quite stacks up to autumn.

With the cooling air temperatures and changing of the leaves comes some of the most stable weather and water levels of the year. At the same time, falling water temperatures draw an enormous migration of bass and their forage into shallow, even predictable areas. Bass seem to anticipate the approach of winter by gorging themselves during this time.

(Opposite page) AFTER BEING lethargic in summertime, bass become active again in the fall as temperatures begin to drop, says Bill Dance.

"Fall is a time when everything seems to come alive," praises Bill Dance, perhaps America's most popular television fishing personality and a former tournament ace with two BASS Angler-of-the-Year awards to his credit. "It is so much more comfortable in the fall for both the fish and the fishermen. And certain techniques in the fall can be extremely reliable. There's a lot to like about fall fishing."

Here, then, are six of the most dependable patterns available to the anglers of autumn.

HEAD FOR THE OXBOWS

Dance, who lives near Memphis, Tenn., has long been a fan of the mighty Mississippi River and its oxbows loaded with largemouth — particularly in early fall, when the water is still hot.

"Even when the days are still scorching, the oxbows are the ticket," Dance says. "There are hundreds of Mississippi River oxbows from St. Louis to Baton Rouge, and countless oxbows

Pro Profile
BILL DANCE
Hometown: Collierville, Tenn.
Birthdate: 10-7-1940

BASS Career Highlights
Tournament Titles: 7 (1970 All American, 1970 Texas National, 1970 Rebel Invitational, 1969 All American, 1968 Dixie Invitational, 1968 All American, 1968 Rebel Invitational)
Times in the Classic: 8
Times in the Money: 54
Total Weight: 1,627 lbs.
Career Winnings: $57,134.42
Avg. Per Tournament: $732.49

Bill Dance is recognized as one of the early pioneers of modern bass fishing. The legendary angler is recognized as the sport's top educator when it comes to seasonal patterns.

Water Clarity And Bass

Water clarity is an important factor to consider when stalking largemouth bass in the fall.

"Baitfish gravitate toward dingier water when given a choice, especially during the early part of the migration," says CITGO Bassmaster University instructor Curt Lytle. "The dingier water is richer in plankton, so the shad and bass are near the surface."

Plankton are tiny aquatic organisms that float throughout the water column and serve as the primary forage for shad. Clear water, notes Lytle, tends to scatter the plankton top to bottom, and baitfish can be anywhere.

"With plankton near the surface, the baitfish move shallower, and the bass are right behind them," he adds.

Three time Busch BASS Angler of the Year Kevin VanDam says he always seeks stained water during the fall.

"Dirty water makes the fall pattern happen quicker," says VanDam. "It positions the fish shallower and tighter to the cover, so they're not roaming around as much. That makes them easier to target."

When stained water isn't available, anglers must change their tactics. Although the fish will relate somewhat to cover, they are likely to be on the move.

"That's when you have to use fast moving baits to keep bass from getting a good look at your lures, and you have to make long casts to keep from spooking the fish," explains VanDam. "Lure size and color become a lot more critical when the fish are feeding primarily by sight."

Former CITGO Bassmaster Classic champion Davy Hite believes water clarity becomes less of an issue when the bait is present and acting normal.

"I won a fall tournament on the Mississippi River when it was muddy," he explains. "However, I found a pocket of clearer water, and the bait and fish were stacked in there."

Later in the fall, muddy water is a deterrent. As any experienced angler will tell you, cold, muddy water is the bane of bass fishing.

"Bass are more aggressive in clear, cold water than they are in cold, muddy water," adds Kentucky pro Mark Menendez. "They're definitely feeding by sight in the late fall more than any other time of the year."

During this time of low water, fish relate to sand points, ledges and flats adjacent to deeper water. To take advantage of the conditions, Dance relies on a 1/2-ounce lipless crankbait and a chartreuse 3/8-ounce spinnerbait.

"You can use those baits to cover a vast amount of cover in a short period of time," declares Dance, "especially when the fish are shallow. During this time, it's usually unproductive to fish any deeper than that because of low oxygen levels."

A slow retrieve is usually critical. As the water cools down, you can speed up your retrieve.

CHANNELING FOR BASS

Experienced fishermen know that much of the best fishing in the fall occurs in major creeks, which are major routes followed by gamefish and baitfish alike. As in spring, they have certain major stopping points along the way.

Instead of following their spawning instincts, fall bass chase baitfish into the backs of creeks. Look for them on the edges of channels, close to feeding flats. Bass congregate along any irregular feature in the channel, such as a channel bend featuring scattered stumps, rocks, logs and the like.

Pros search out such spots in 25 to 30 feet of water in late September — the initial phase of the fall migration — where they try to locate schools of bass and baitfish. To imitate the latter, jig a 3/4-ounce spoon vertically over the structure.

As the water continues to cool in October and November, follow the fish farther into the creek, casting crankbaits into shallow feeding grounds in depths 8 to 15 feet. A medium retrieve is best, and it's important to pay particular attention to every piece of cover. It's not unusual to catch several bass on one particular stump.

SCHOOLING BASS

Anyone who has ever experienced the frenzied feeding of schooling bass will know that fall is prime time to be on the water. "This is just about the most fun you can have with a fishing rod," says one schooling bass fan. Schooling occurs

on smaller rivers. They really hold fish during this time of year."

Most oxbows are formed as rivers snake their way through lowland landscapes, cutting new channels and leaving behind horseshoe-shaped lakes. In early fall, most of the bass activity occurs in shallow water.

TO COAX bass out of deep water during the early stages of the fall migration, jig a spoon around channel bends that feature cover.

when open water bass corral schools of baitfish and herd them to the surface. Be alert for the sounds and sights of gluttonous bass attacking bait on the surface. Where gulls hang out, seeing birds diving to pick up injured shad is a sure sign of feeding fish. Then, the race is on to reach the school before it sounds.

Time is of the essence when chasing schooling fish. In the fall, keep several rods on the front deck. Rig them with tailspinners, topwaters, spoons and other shadlike baits you can cast a long way.

Once the school disappears, you might hook larger bass (schoolers typically are small) by swimming a jig through the area. Quality-size bass sometimes hang near the bottom in 10 to 12 feet of water.

THE GRASS BASS OF FALL

In the fall on lakes with well-defined grass points, huge schools of feisty bass gather in these obvious places. Pros seek out any points created by hydrilla beds on shallow flats located near deeper water, such as on a channel edge. Action typically is shallow, with big fish prowling the 2- to 5-foot zone. The fish will set up on a point of grass and live in that area throughout the fall, leaving it only to feed along a nearby flat.

This is the time to fling a buzzbait or spinnerbait over and through the shallow vegetation. When the bass are especially active, they might hit crankbaits, particularly the lipless variety, fished across the top or along the outside edges of the weeds.

This is also a deadly pattern in Northern waters, where smallmouth roam in wolf packs. There, however, the action occurs much earlier in the fall, and the productive weed points tend to be somewhat deeper — 5 to 18 feet deep, depending on water clarity and weed depth. To catch them, fish a midrange crankbait parallel to the grassline. As temperatures cool, try a jig-and-pig in the same places.

DOCKS AND RAMPS

Two of Bill Dance's favorite autumn bass haunts are among the most obvious — and over-looked — of all: boat docks and ramps.

Dock fishing can be productive throughout the year, but Dance contends that early to midfall is a prime time to target wooden piers.

The most productive fall docks are positioned near deep water and possess accessories like floodlights and pole holders, which indicate dock owners are anglers and may have submerged brush-piles.

KNOWN FOR HIS "fall" fishing, Dance believes there may be no better time of year to pursue America's favorite gamefish.

"Believe it or not, most anglers actually drive over one of the very best bass holding structures every time they launch their boats, particularly in the early fall: the ramp itself," Dance says. "A boat ramp provides a clear, hard bottom where there is no cover to hide baitfish. When schools of shad cruise along and around the ramp, they are easy pickings for bass."

Early in the season, Dance enjoys some surprisingly good results while fishing at night around well-lit public ramps. The light attracts baitfish to the concrete bottom section. In this situation, the Tennessee pro employs a black spinnerbait, a black jig-and-pig, or a dark-colored plastic worm.

"It's amazing the number of bass you can catch fishing boat ramps at night, particularly in early fall," Dance concludes. "And don't overlook ramps in the daytime, either."

Armed with the never-fail patterns provided by our experts, the average angler can squeeze every bit of the fun out of fall fishing. And, after all, autumn is the time to celebrate bass fishing at its best.

DROP SHOTTING with 1/4-ounce and heavier sinkers will produce quality fish during wintertime.

RELIABLE WINTER BASS PATTERNS
Seven great places to find bass in cold weather

I T'S MID-NOVEMBER 1999 — the final day of the California Bassmaster Invitational — and Lake Oroville is playing tough. The spotted bass for which this 15,500-acre impoundment is best known seem to have shrunk to barely legal size, and the largemouth apparently have taken an early holiday vacation. Neil Howard, with 21 pounds, 13 ounces, holds an 8-ounce lead over Aaron Martens.

California pro Mike O'Shea starts the last round in 23rd place, with a total of 18-4. He knows he has a lot of ground to make up, and to do that, he's going to have to rely almost entirely on pure winter fishing instincts. Without hesitation, he heads to a rockpile located near the junction of two creeks, and starts drop shotting a plastic worm into water 60 feet deep.

By day's end, he's culled a five bass limit weighing 13 pounds, 15 ounces — the heaviest catch by anyone all week — and he claims second place, just 9 ounces behind winner Aaron Martens.

"In Western lakes, winter techniques often depend more on the impoundment than on the weather, since so many of the reservoirs are deep and rocky, and the bass tend to be in deeper water throughout the year," explains O'Shea.

"Sometimes when the weather turns cold at a lake like Oroville, you have to fish some pretty astounding depths, but if you can find the bass, you can catch them."

The depths O'Shea feels comfortable fishing contrast sharply with the winter techniques used by BASS pros who concentrate on the much shallower lakes of the

(Opposite page)
FISH BENDS of creek channels in the middle and lower portions of a lake during wintertime.

Pro Profile
MIKE O'SHEA
Hometown: Thousand Oaks, Calif.
Birthdate: 5-4-1961

BASS Career Highlights
Tournament Titles: Has not yet won a Bassmaster title.
Times in the Classic: 1
Times in the Money: 17
Total Weight: 600 lbs.
Career Winnings: $66,417
Avg. Per Tournament: $2,290.24

Mike O'Shea is a wintertime wonder when bass are lethargic during cold months.

FISH ALONG tapering main lake points first when attempting to pattern wintertime largemouth, says western pro Mike O'Shea.

South. Texas guide and Tournament Trail pro Sean Hoernke always looks first for a shallow bite in less than 10 feet of water, even when he has clients out on Lake Ray Roberts, which receives some of the most severe weather in north Texas.

"In this part of the country, the No. 1 factor affecting winter bass fishing is the weather," says Hoernke, whose résumé includes a fifth place finish at a Missouri Bassmaster Invitational. "The first thing I want to know on any fishing trip this time of year is what the weather has been doing for the past several days, because that will tell me what the bass are doing now."

Because they face such different geographical conditions in the areas they fish, Hoernke and O'Shea attack cold weather bass in different ways. Together, however, their accumulated knowledge can provide a much needed boost to any fisherman having trouble when the water is cold. O'Shea's approach should not be limited to Western waters, nor should Hoernke's be restricted to the South.

Following are their recommendations for establishing productive bass patterns in winter.

START WITH POINTS

"The first thing I try in winter is a point on the main lake, because most Western lakes have a lot of them," says O'Shea, who has been fishing Western tournaments for many years. He uses one of two lures on points: a 3/4-ounce spinnerbait with No. 5 gold willowleaf and No. 2 silver Colorado blades, or a No. 6 deep diving crankbait.

"I probably rely on the crankbait the most at first because I cover water that may be as shallow as 3 feet and work down to about 15 feet," he says. "I fan-cast the point using erratic retrieves, and I try to keep the crankbait hitting the bottom as much as possible."

At depths greater than 15 feet, O'Shea changes to a 3/4-ounce spider jig (a lighter jig if brushy cover is present), moves his boat shallow and starts crawling the jig up the slope from deeper water.

TRY RIPRAP NEXT

If the points don't produce, O'Shea usually moves to his second winter fishing option, rock riprap, which can be productive on virtually any type of impoundment or river system. He prefers the long walls that are often present at dams and around bridge crossings.

"I think riprap initially attracts baitfish better than it does bass, because the gaps in the rocks offer some protection and shelter," notes O'Shea, "and on sunny days, the rocks hold heat. It doesn't take the bass long to find the bait. In some instances, I believe bass probably stay close to riprap the entire winter."

The first line of business in fishing riprap is defining a depth zone bass are using, and for this, O'Shea uses his crankbait. Fishing with 10-pound-test line and a deep diving crankbait, he generally begins at one end of the rocks and makes his casts straight in so the lure will cover water from 2 to nearly 15 feet.

"Once you catch a fish, and certainly after you catch several, you should be able to start defining a

FISH BLUFFS adjacent to creek channels where bass have immediate access to deep water during cold-water months.

depth where the bass are holding," he explains. "At that point, you can begin casting parallel along the riprap so your lure works that depth longer.

"Although bass can be anywhere along a wall of rocks, I especially like to fish corners, or anywhere there is some type of change in the rocks."

HEAVY DROP SHOTTING

Although many consider drop shotting to be a light tackle technique, some Western pros, like O'Shea, regularly rig with 1/2-ounce and heavier sinkers — even on 6-pound-test line — for deep winter bass. That's what O'Shea was doing that last day at Lake Oroville. His lure choice then was a 4 1/2-inch RoboWorm.

"When you're fishing that deep, a heavy weight is important because it takes the lure to the bottom faster," he explains. "It doesn't have any effect on your lure's action because you're using a near-vertical presentation and the sinker stays on the bottom.

"One of the real differences in deep, heavy drop shotting is that we may put our small plastic lures 3 or 4 feet up the line, rather than just 8 or 12 inches like you do in shallower water. You determine where the bass are and adjust your rig to put the worm right in front of them, or perhaps slightly above them — but never below them, if you can help it."

The depth bass are holding is known as the "activity zone," and O'Shea finds it by carefully studying his depthfinder. In the summer, the activity zone is often just above the thermocline, and it shows up well on electronics because few fish will be below it. Idling slowly across deep water in a lake will usually show the thermocline fairly quickly.

In the winter, you won't find a thermocline, but an activity

zone still exists. It probably is somewhat related to water temperatures at various levels, but it also has a great deal to do with structure. By watching his depthfinder as he motors across his fishing area, O'Shea finds the depth at which most bass seem to be holding — the activity zone — and then tries to find structure at that depth.

"Another way to find the activity zone is by following prominent structure out to progressively deeper water and looking for bass as you go," the California pro acknowledges. "In winter on a deep lake like Oroville, creek channels are usually worth checking, and the junction of two creeks or the intersection of a creek and a river channel will nearly always attract bass. You can find places like this on a map, then pinpoint them once you're on the water."

Drop shotting in deep water takes a more sensitive touch than in shallow water, so O'Shea tries to make his presentations as nearly vertical as possible; he doesn't try to "walk" the sinker around structure or cover. Once the weight is on the bottom, he shakes his rod to make the worm quiver without moving

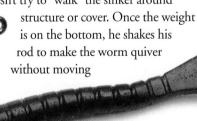

KEEP DROP SHOT rigs in the thermocline by using electronics to find the deep water "activity zone."

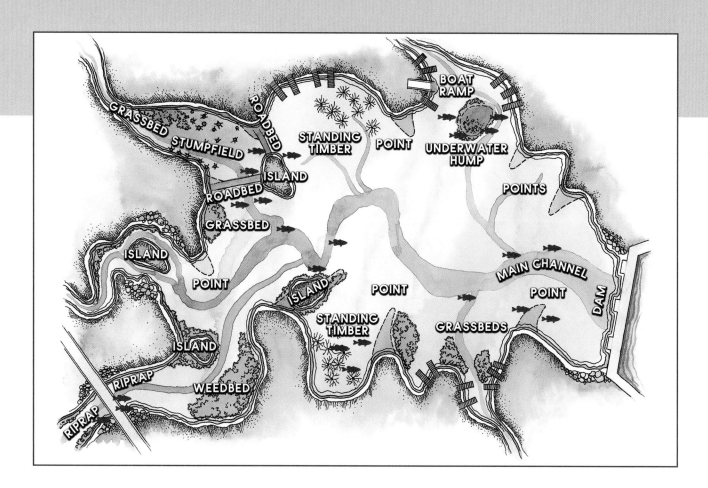

the sinker. Most strikes are seen, rather than felt, as the line begins moving away.

In the generally shallow lakes of the South, fellow pro Sean Hoernke, like O'Shea, begins his winter fishing days by looking first for a shallow bite. A succession of slightly warmer days, especially if the weather has been unusually cold, may cause bass to move up from deeper water, so wherever he's fishing, he concentrates on vertical rather than sloping structure.

THE VEGETATION FACTOR

Thick grassbeds disappear in winter on most lakes, but some Southern reservoirs will have plenty of vegetation hidden beneath the surface. After several sunny days in a row, bass often move onto shallower flats, intersecting the edges of the weedbeds. The best spots offer easy access to deep water.

Most anglers fish fairly slowly, thinking bass are too lethargic to chase a fast moving lure. Instead, offer them a fast moving lipless crankbait or even a buzzbait churning over the grass. You might draw a reaction strike from a bass that simply can't refuse your noisy lure.

KEY SPOTS for winter bass include any vertical structure or cover with deep water access nearby. Also look for green, growing vegetation on grassy lakes.

The effectiveness of a 3/4-ounce red Rat-L-Trap is legendary in late winter/early spring on grassy lakes, such as Sam Rayburn and Toledo Bend in Texas. What isn't so well-known is how effective these lipless crankbaits can be in the dead of winter, especially adjacent to the weedlines.

SPOON FISHING TIMBER

Standing timber provides prime cover for winter bass, and because you can see trees above the waterline, it's fairly easy to find and fish effectively, says Hoernke.

Look for the largest trees, which seem to hold bigger bass and which normally are located along the edges of old creek channels. Standing timber along the steeper outside bend of a creek channel, is almost guaranteed to hold bass.

Tie on a straight, heavy jigging spoon weighing 1/2 to 3/4 ounce, and drop it straight down along the tree trunk. For a different appearance and

IN LAKES with standing timber, the fish will hold on the edges of old creek channel bends. Catch them by jigging a spoon in the treetops.

softer feel — as well as a slightly slower fall — some pros slip a spoon inside a tube lure. It produces less flash, and it simply gives bass something different to look at.

The key to spoon fishing is letting the lure flutter back down with no resistance, which means lowering your rod tip at the same speed the spoon is falling. If the line is too tight, the spoon won't have any action, but if you let it fall on a completely slack line, you don't have any control over it.

Hoernke recommends working all around a tree, popping the spoon off the bottom, 2 to 4 feet at a pop, and watch for the lure to stop falling unexpectedly. That means you've either hit a branch or had a hit from a bass. Don't take a chance — set the hook.

CRANKING ROADBEDS

When cranking a roadbed, Hoernke is looking for a reaction bite, which doesn't depend upon a fish's interest in feeding. A jig or Carolina rigged soft plastic represents something to eat, and bass aren't hungry often enough in winter to take those lures.

Depending on the depth, you'll need a crankbait capable of diving 20 to 25 feet — the maximum range for a lure on a long cast. Pros look for roadbeds along the edges of channels, and they cast parallel to the road, starting first on the edges.

Roadbeds are depicted on many lake maps, but they can only be pinpointed with the aid of a depthfinder. Look for any depth changes, no matter how slight, that might represent a roadbed bordered by ditches on each side. When fishing older reservoirs, remember that the ditches might be filled with silt and won't show up prominently on sonar.

A roadbed is capable of holding big schools of fish, but expect them to be concentrated in a small place. Sometimes you can even see them with your depthfinder, and most of the time they're going to be near some type of change in the roadbed.

CURRENT STABILITY

When weather conditions are unstable, look for steady current, because it will offer the most stable conditions on the lake at that time. This often means a long run up a lake's major tributary, sometimes to the dam impounding the next up-river lake.

Current in these types of places offers the chance to fish for resident bass that might never venture close to the main lake. Their world is dominated by moving water — not necessarily water temperature, and their actions can be fairly predictable.

In these conditions, Hoernke recommends a 3/8- or 1/2-ounce jig-and-pig, a 1/2-ounce tandem willowleaf spinnerbait or a shallow running, wide-wobbling crankbait. Concentrate on anything that breaks the current; including laydowns, logjams, rocks and other cover.

Expect to find bass positioned right on the edge of the current. Aim your casts slightly upstream of the target, and let the current carry your lure into the eddy and beside your target. This involves fishing fairly shallow around visible cover, and it's something most anglers can relate to. If you can find the right conditions, you can catch a lot of bass, even in the coldest water.

RIVER PATTERNS

Raging rapids, swirling eddies
and shallow pools —
all places current-dwelling bass
are found . . .

YEAR-ROUND
RIVER PATTERNS

Current is the key to unlocking a river's puzzle

RIVER FISHING bears little resemblance to the lake and reservoir experiences with which most of us grew up. The environment that houses these bass is so radically different that much of what we learned by fishing more stagnant bodies of water often doesn't apply to moving water.

Yet the ability to successfully read rivers and locate the resident bass usually isn't nearly as difficult

as it might seem. In fact, river bass can be patterned on a seasonal basis, much like bass in a lake.

"It's a whole different ball game from reservoir or lake fishing," says Kentucky pro Mike Auten. "There are times when a river will fish like a lake, or a lake will fish like a river, but for the most part it is a totally different way of fishing."

Locating river bass can be considerably easier than their more calm water counterparts if there is any

current. That is because bass will relate to obvious places along the river. All of these spots have a common denominator — they provide a break in the current and an ambush point for bass.

Regardless of the season, an inexperienced river fisherman would do well to concentrate on current breaks that include points, bars, riffles, boulders, fallen trees, pilings, wing dams (jetties), bridges and major bends in the river. Any object large enough to create an area of calm water behind it can be home to a river bass (or an entire school).

"With river fishing, you have two factors that work in your favor — current and confinement," Auten explains. "Current tells you how the bass are going to be positioned. They are not going to be out fighting the current. They will be behind some current break, facing the current and waiting for baitfish or crawfish to be flushed past them.

"The biggest factor may be confinement. You've got less area contained within the banks of a river that you have to be concerned with. It is not like a lake, where fish might live out in the middle in 12 to 60 feet of water. Rivers condense everything into a smaller area, and there is a lot of visual structure that you don't have in some lakes. Even the best river fishermen simply concentrate on visible cover that provides a break in the current."

Water flow is the very basis of river fishing.

Radio telemetry studies by fisheries researchers have shown that river bass have a significantly smaller range of movement than those living in calmer water. It is believed that current is responsible for this smaller home range.

"River fish are always more aggressive," adds North Carolina pro Guy Eaker. "With that moving water, the fish is always in a position where it is waiting for food to come by.

"I think river fish are quicker to hit a bait. They have to be more aggressive because of the swiftness of the water. A lake bass holding on a long point, a bar or a ledge can examine a bait for a long time without worrying about it escaping. But a river bass hiding behind a rock has to react instantly at the sight of a baitfish, or it will wash right past. That's what makes them easier to catch than lake fish."

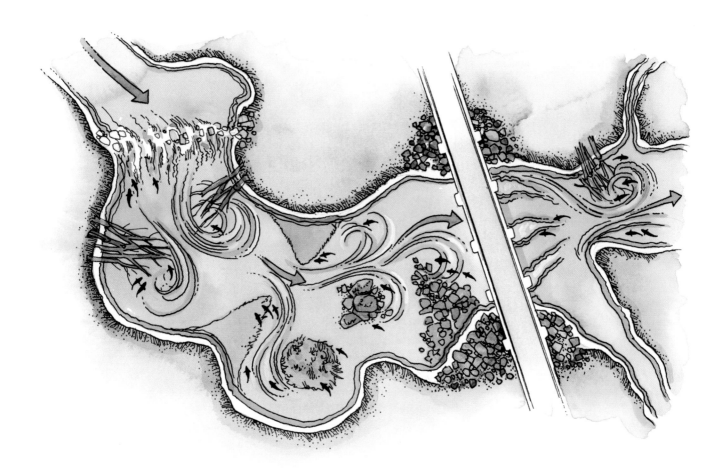

Just as current can actually pinpoint bass' location by positioning them in obvious places, lack of current will destroy that precious bit of predictability. With no flow, river bass tend to scatter,

WHEN USING crankbaits for river fishing, make them run into cover, like boulders, that disrupt the flow of current.

no longer hampered by (or attracted to) fast water.

The fast-and-furious fishing of yesterday can be completely transformed a day later by a variety of factors, ranging from natural (rainfall runoff) to man-made (power generation). That instability inherent in river fishing is a major reason veteran anglers incorporate seasonal patterns into their daily strategy.

And that includes current.

"The desirability of current changes, especially in the winter and summer," states Randy Howell, a top young pro who grew up in the Carolinas and now makes his home in Alabama. "In the winter, I try to avoid the current and concentrate more in the stillwater areas. The fish will

still stay close to the current for the food source, but they won't be in the current.

"In the summer, the fish are going to stay real close to the flow, or almost in the flow. They're going to be moving and feeding a lot more often than they do in the winter."

Howell and fellow Alabama river expert Gerald Swindle offer this season-by-season guide to river fishing:

Winter — "When it gets real cold, the baitfish will move out of the creeks and tributaries and onto the main river, where the fishing can be surprisingly good," claims Howell, a past CITGO Bassmaster Classic presented by Busch qualifier. "Then, a jig is your best bet, especially when it's flipped around big trees, steep drops, bluff banks and such.

"That's when you catch the bigger bass in the river, because it's cold and the fish are lethargic and not moving around a lot. I fish a 1/2-ounce jig and a plastic chunk around rocks and other objects along channel

BASS FEED when current flows in river systems controlled by dams. Look for them to hold tight to cover, such as ledges, when the water is moving.

banks to catch big fish when it's cold."

Howell's secondary wintertime pattern involves slow rolling a 3/4-ounce spinnerbait around any submerged wood located in deep bends and channel swings in the river.

Swindle, who learned to fish rivers while floating in an inner tube as a youngster, concentrates on fallen trees in the main river — particularly laydowns large enough to extend out into deep water. This is the kind of cover cold water bass will relate to throughout the day as the water warms. He flips

WORK A SURFACE minnow in river systems when the bass are seen chasing bait in current breaks.

SINCE SMALLMOUTH spawn before other bass species, early spring is an excellent time for catching top-water bronzebacks.

FLIP A JIG-AND-CHUNK into isolated cover located on long points extending into the river and adjacent to feeder creeks.

current," he explains. "In other words, if the river is moving due north, I look for a creek that runs south. This keeps the current from flowing out of the river into that pocket. The water stays in there longer and warms faster.

"You can take a temperature gauge and check these pockets that go opposite the current, and I promise you the surface temperature will rise 2 or 3 degrees every time."

Swindle scores handsomely with a Lucky Craft Pointer jerkbait on the prespawners and bedding bass in these unique areas.

Howell also searches for warmer backwater areas, where he covers a lot of water with a spinnerbait, floating worm or soft jerkbait in search of prespawners.

Spring — As the spawn approaches, Howell moves even shallower in the backwater areas, where the big female bass settle in. He can most likely be found working the shorelines by skipping a brightly colored floating worm or soft jerkbait beneath overhanging brush and tree limbs.

Late spring — Immediate postspawn brings some excellent topwater action on rivers, according to Howell. He works a buzzbait above any cover or objects positioned in the bedding area. It is also a time when you can see bass moving around these areas as they protect their fry. These fish are highly susceptible to a soft jerkbait or floating worm.

"Once they stop following the fry around, the fish will just lie down on the bottom," Howell reveals. "That's when I start flipping a big worm and concentrating on big (submerged) trees that stick out from the bank into, say, 10 feet of water."

Summer — "My summer pattern is pretty simple," relates Swindle, who prefers to pitch a fast falling 5/8-ounce jig during the warmest times on the river. "I work upriver, looking for steeper banks and longer points to fish.

"A lot of times, you will find one key point that runs out 50 or 60 yards from the bank, and you'll be surprised at the number of fish holding on that point. The key

these trees methodically with a big (5/8- to 3/4-ounce) jig.

Early spring — At the first hint of spring, Swindle automatically heads for the lower end of the river, where he targets small pockets and creeks. That's where the warmest water usually will be found. "I always look for pockets and creeks that run opposite to the river

is to start in a good spawning area and then look around the mouths of creeks and along the river bank in the vicinity. Those bass won't move any farther than they have to after spawning to settle into their summer places."

Summer is when Howell is drawn to deep river bends and steeper banks that harbor trees or brush. He will bob and weave his way through the brush with a crankbait. When that doesn't work, he fishes a plastic worm.

Fall — "Usually, a river system is at its best in the fall, because there is always a little bit of current flowing through. And once you figure out where the fish are positioned, they will bite," Howell says. "The fish will be hanging on the edge of the current.

"My favorite technique in the fall is flipping a jig in trees and blowdowns. I try to look for isolated stuff — not the banks with the 'pretty' trees that everybody fishes. Find the banks that have just one or two logs. If it breaks the current, a bass will get behind it. Drop a jig in there, or bring a crankbait, like a square-lipped Bandit, through it, and you will get bit."

As the season progresses, Howell follows the baitfish as they migrate to the rear of creeks — a classic fall pattern. This is a fun time to be a bass fisherman, a period when aggressive largemouth can be caught on practically any lure and in water as shallow as 6 to 8 inches.

"Fall fishing is fantastic in rivers," says Swindle, another Classic qualifier. "That's generally when the water is the coolest and fastest. The rivers are usually high, so you can get farther up in them, where you're going to find a shade pattern along the banks. The water stays cooler, and the baitfish get real active. That means the bass will be active, too."

This is topwater time for Swindle, who relies on Lucky Craft G-Splash plugs and buzzbaits.

There is nothing quite like river fishing for bass. By taking the current into consideration and arming themselves with some seasonal knowledge, anglers of all experience levels can take advantage of all the river has to offer.

Fly Fishing Tidal Rivers

King Montgomery, a guide on the Potomac River, believes the fly rod to be a valuable tool when gunning for bass on tidal waterways, especially during the warmer months.

"I fly fish tidal rivers because doing so is both fun and effective. Plus, the summer months are topwater time, particularly early or late in the day and under low light conditions," Montgomery emphasizes. Not that fly fishing bassers are chained to surface baits. In fact, flies can imitate what the guide calls the "four basic food groups of bass" — surface, subsurface, middepth and bottom prey — with startling accuracy.

And since many tidal rivers are less than 10 feet in depth, the fly rodder typically does not face the difficulty of plumbing the depths, as fly fishermen often experience in lakes.

The key to determining where to fish in summer is understanding bait movement. America's tidal rivers are typically quite fertile and host an abundance of minnow and shad species. These baitfish move a great deal during the day, according to tide movements and light penetration. Of course, the bass reposition as their forage does.

"In summer, I begin early in the day with a weight-forward floating line for casting poppers or hair bugs on a 7 1/2- or 9-foot knotless tapered leader," the guide says. "I work them in and around beds and deeper water; in tidal rivers that may mean vegetation in 3 feet of water next to an area 5 feet deep.

"As the sun rises, I still remain around the grass and pads, but I present floater-divers and streamers in water between 1 foot and 5 feet. I use a short 4- to 6-foot knotless tapered sinking leader for the streamers," he says.

As the day progresses, Montgomery moves to boat docks, bridge pilings and main river grassbeds. Here he uses sink-tip line with 4- to 6-foot leaders and hair jigs.

TIDAL BASS move shallow to feed as the water rises on the incoming tide. The fish move back out and then hold tight to cover on the falling tide.

UNLOCKING TIDAL WATERS
Catching huge bass in the ebb and flow

KEEP IT SIMPLE," Robert Lee advises about fishing tidal waters, "or you'll get confused real easy."

Bass fishermen are wise to pay attention when Lee talks about tidal bass strategies. The young California pro has multiple BASS wins to his credit, and all came on the tidal waters of California's legendary San Joaquin Delta. In one of those events, Lee amassed a three day total weight of 78 pounds, 3 ounces, which was a BASS record at the time.

Tidal fisheries tend to overwhelm anglers, and it's easy to understand why. Current can flow in two opposite directions, and water levels commonly fluctuate several feet with every tide cycle. Salinity, which affects forage species and bass habitat, can vary according to past weeks' weather patterns, and in some locations, wind conditions can override tidal cycles.

Complicating things further, many tidal fisheries spread over thousands of acres and may include multiple main river channels, forks off

those channels, hidden lakes, tidal creeks, backwater sloughs, canals and more. The San Joaquin Delta, for example, actually includes the lower ends of four major rivers.

Lee begins with one basic rule, which his entire tidal waters strategy almost always revolves around: "When the water comes up, the fish move up. When the water goes back down, the fish move back down."

In tidal water tournaments, Lee always likes to find a group of fish and stay in one main area, following the fish up and down with the changing tides. He fishes "reaction baits," including topwater lures, spinnerbaits and crankbaits, through the upper half of each tidal cycle, throwing them around vegetation and flooded shoreline cover. As the water goes down, he drops back to deeper channels and fishes with worms, jigs and deeper running crankbaits.

"Water fluctuations affect everything on waters that connect with the ocean," says Shaw Grigsby, who grew up fishing tidal rivers along Florida's Gulf Coast and who has fished virtually every major tidal system in the country. "The stage and direction of the tide are things you really pay attention to, and you plan everything based on the tides."

Grigsby notes that one day's great location and pattern — with the bass holding in shallow lily pads — may not do a bit of good a few days later at the same time. "Those pads may not even have water under them then," he said.

Running down the Suwannee to fish some canals for tidal bass last year, Grigsby pointed out pads along the way that were essentially high and dry. He said that those same spots would have fish in them when the tide came up. Later in the afternoon, after the tide flooded those flats, he flipped the same pads and pulled several nice bass from the area that had been high and dry only hours earlier.

Tidal waters aren't difficult, according to Grigsby. In fact, bass become very predictable once fishermen figure out how bass behave according to conditions. "Because the tides control everything, fish in these systems are far less affected by fronts than are fish in reservoirs," he says.

However, fishermen cannot just cast at everything that looks like bass cover and expect to catch fish consistently. Tidal fluctuations affect not only which cover the bass will use, but also how they will relate to that cover and how aggressively they will feed.

"When the water's down, the fish will be near more vertical edges, which have deeper water on them," Grigsby explains. "When it's flowing out of small creeks, they'll sit just out of that current. When the tide changes directions, they'll move to the opposite sides of points. Those are the types of little things you have to pay attention to."

Grigsby also suggests that anglers break vast

Pro Profile
ROBERT LEE
Hometown: Angels Camp, Calif.
Birthdate: 5-19-1968

BASS Career Highlights
Tournament Titles: 4 (2003 California Tour Pro, 2001 California Invitational, 1999 California Invitational, 1997 California Invitational)
Times in the Classic: 2
Times in the Money: 21
Total Weight: 995 lbs., 5 ozs.
Career Winnings: $257,087
Avg. Per Tournament: $6,270.41

Robert Lee won four consecutive BASS titles held on California's San Joaquin Delta, qualifying him as the tour's tidewater bass guru.

FIND A GROUP OF BASS and stay in one main area, following the fish up and down with the changing tides, advises tidal expert Robert Lee.

tidal fisheries into categories, such as main rivers, creeks, canals, sloughs and such to help the patterning process. "Tidal fish are very pattern-oriented," Grigsby adds, "so you have to eliminate areas where you don't catch fish."

Grigsby has learned what cover should hold fish and how they should relate to it, based on conditions, so if he doesn't get hit in likely places on main river banks, he typically moves fairly quickly to creeks, canals or some other area.

Louisiana BASS pro Sam Swett, who cut his angling teeth fishing the Louisiana Delta, plans his entire day based on when and where the tides will be at what stage. As he dissects coastal bass fisheries, Swett looks at tidal waters more in terms of "incoming vs. outgoing" than as "high vs. low."

Given the option, Swett would prefer to fish outgoing tides, but since a pro doesn't have that choice on tournament day, he has learned the best ways to approach tidal waters no matter which way the water is flowing.

"High to low is generally best," Swett reiterates. "High tides flood the backwaters of a system. As the water goes back out, I focus on ditches, canals and feeder creeks that drain those backwaters, fishing in the current created by those areas flowing into the river."

Swett generally throws small, shallow diving crankbaits and soft plastics in these areas. He Texas rigs the plastics, generally using a light enough weight so that the current will move the bait a bit every time he lifts it off the bottom.

"The bass are looking for food being swept out in that current," he says.

For rising tides, Swett prefers steep banks, often along the main river. "When the water is going up, those fish seem to get right against the steepest banks they can find," he explains.

Swett also looks for steep banks in the very backs of any sloughs he can get up into. "I go as far back as I can get, and look for those steep banks. It's not that the bass aren't on the flatter areas, too. They are. You just can't get far enough back to fish them."

For either location, Swett typically turns to topwaters (stickbaits and poppers) or jerkbaits for fishing the rising water.

The most difficult time, most tidal anglers agree, is during "slack tides," when the tides are turning around and there are no defined currents. "Nothing holds fish in any particular place during that time," Swett says. "So, they roam a lot and don't concentrate at all."

To contend with roaming fish, Swett moves quickly during slack tides, covering a lot of bank and a variety of shoreline types with fast moving baits. Some of the same crankbaits he likes at other times come into play now, but he also makes a lot of casts with a lipless crankbait.

Throughout the tides, all three pros fish a lot of crankbaits in tidal waters. Grigsby points to shallow running crankbaits as being the puzzle pieces needed for almost all tidal situations, with the latter running the deepest and being best-suited for low water fishing. He likes a lot of red or blue, both of which imitate crustaceans.

Grigsby also spends a lot of time throwing a spinnerbait in tidal waters, usually throwing a small bait and sticking with Colorado blades. He relies heavily on 1/4- or 3/16-ounce spinnerbaits, including one that sports four Colorado blades.

"I love them with Colorado blades. I think the round blades remind the fish of the backs of little crabs," Grigsby says. For the same reason, he likes spinnerbait color patterns that have a lot of blue and purple in them.

Robert Lee tries to imitate crawfish with almost everything he throws. "I really think that in most tidal fisheries, bass key on crawfish 90 percent of the year. Big fish really key on crawfish. That's why I throw a lot of jigs and crawfish-colored crankbaits," he says.

A final, important consideration about tidal waters is that while all have certain common denominators, every system is unique. Some consist basically of a river and its forks, creeks and canals. Others spread across massive marshy deltas. Additionally, anglers have to determine how far upstream the tides affect the system, and how strong those tides are.

The San Joaquin Delta and most major river systems along the Atlantic coast have strong tidal flows, and the water moves in and out twice per

Tidewater Opinions

Many of the best bass rivers in America are tidal by nature, meaning they fluctuate once or twice a day, like clockwork. As a result, tidal fishing still baffles both the weekend angler and the pro. Many of the most elite bass fishermen in the country admit that they are largely lost when it comes to tidewater fishing.

Shaw Grigsby

"Tidal fishing can be a complete mystery to people who are unfamiliar with it," says Florida pro Shaw Grigsby, who grew up fishing the tidal fluctuations of the Suwannee and St. Johns rivers. "It can be confusing, even to the very best fishermen."

The almost constantly changing conditions of a tidewater system can make a certain spot red-hot for a few minutes, and then render it worthless for the rest of the day.

Tidal conditions can exist on river systems more than 100 miles from the coast, ebbing and flowing according to the moon's position. Tides on most inland rivers change once a day, featuring a high tide that inundates the marshes, and a low tide that drains the shoreline.

"The key to tidal fishing is being in the right place at the right time," explains BASS veteran pro Woo Daves, a tidewater expert. "It is a game of moving regularly from area to area to take advantage of the tide as it changes throughout the river."

The low tide eliminates much of the habitat that bass use — particularly along the shoreline and in the marshes — forcing them to congregate in obvious places. Those places include any object (tree, boulder or shoal) that provides a break in the current, as well as the entrances to feeder creeks where baitfish are flushed out as the water drains into the main river.

With the presence of moving water, bass will usually be facing the current to ambush baitfish and other food sources as they are swept downstream. That is vital knowledge for making the proper lure presentation. But it is important to remember that once the tide changes, the bass will move to the opposite side of the current break to adjust to the new direction of the flowing water. Because of that, bass will often be concentrated between a pair of fallen trees or large rocks.

Tide charts pinpoint the times when these river bass are most likely to be actively feeding — information that is mostly guesswork for stillwater anglers.

"With a tidal system, you have a daily timetable to work with," Daves says. "And you aren't at the mercy of some power company.

"The bass are tuned in to feeding at certain points of the tide, particularly on the outgoing tide, when there is less water and the baitfish get pulled out of the marshes and flooded grass areas. On the incoming tide, as the water gets high, it disperses the baitfish. On some rivers, I think the bass are accustomed to resting on the incoming tide and feeding on the outgoing tide."

Most tidal experts prefer the final 90 minutes of an outgoing tide and the first hour of incoming flow. These situations eliminate water, position bass in obvious places and put them in an active mode.

And the published tide charts tell you when the fishing is likely to be best.

FOLLOWING THE LEADING EDGE of the incoming tide is another option for catching tidewater fish. The object is to hit the hot spots when the high tide is flowing through.

day. Some of those fluctuate only a couple of feet; others vary several feet with every swing of the tides.

The Hudson River has strikingly strong tides and normal fluctuations of 5 or 6 feet, Grigsby points out. "I was fishing down a series of poles on the Hudson as the tide was coming in, pitchin' to fish positioned beside some poles. I came to the end of the row and turned the boat around, and the poles weren't there anymore."

Gulf of Mexico deltas, by way of contrast, have tides that typically fluctuate less than a foot, and they only go in and out once per day. The 12 hour swing is far more gradual, and sustained winds blowing off the ocean can actually overpower the tides and keep the water from ever going out. Similarly, a few days of strong north winds along the northern Gulf Coast can push the water right out to sea and really complicate the bass fishing.

Pros competing in tournaments generally opt for one of two basic strategies for fishing tidal waters. The first, which Lee prefers as his technique of choice, is to pick an area and adjust specific locations and techniques as the tides change. The other is to "run the tides," which refers to running from spot to spot and hitting each when the tide is best for that particular spot.

Running tides can work well on rivers that have strong tides and a lot of well-defined spots along its route. Swett mentions the Potomac as a good example. "You can start around D.C., fishing the best part of the outgoing tide, and then literally run down ahead of the water to fish the best part of the outgoing tide in another spot."

Grigsby says anglers often make "milk runs" on tidal rivers, hitting all their prime spots at just the right time, tide-wise. "Of course, if someone is in that spot when you want to fish it, you can be in trouble, and if your timing gets off, the whole plan might be ruined."

Lee considers running tides pretty risky, for those very reasons. "Plus, you spend too much time running from spot to spot and not enough time fishing," he says.

Tidal-Dock Bass

Many tidewater regions feature an abundance of shoreline development, especially waterfront homes with docks and piers, and these are key spots for catching tidewater bass.

Docks are particularly attractive to bass because many are so long — some nearly 300 yards in length — and are bordered by fertile grassbeds that attract minnows and other bass forage. (The docks are built long enough to reach water deep enough to float boats at low tides.)

Too, old docks are better than new ones, because they often have an abundance of barnacles (which are very efficient line cutters), weeds and deteriorating wood that draws minnows. The more pilings and cross supports under a dock, the better it is. Docks lowest to the water also are preferred by bass because they offer the most shade.

One tip-off to some hot tidewater docks are sailboats or large cruising boats. These boats generally have deep keels, indicating that water around the dock will be fairly deep. Such holes harbor bass, especially in summer during low tides. An abundance of dock pilings nearby helps, too.

When a tide turns and falls, bass often drop off shoreline flats and head to deeper water. Dock fish normally relocate to the deepest pilings, or may even move offshore to ledges or humps.

Catching good-size bass from tidewater docks can be tricky when using standard bass tackle, because of line-cutting barnacles. Fortunately, much tidewater where bass abound is stained dark, so lines testing as much as 20 pounds can be used.

HOW TO FISH BACKWATERS

Reaching these hot spots is worth the effort

IT MUST HAVE BEEN a strange sight. Jay Yelas stood in ankle-deep water 10 miles up the main feeder creek for Illinois' Pool 26 of the Mississippi River, swinging a pick and shovel like a member of a chain gang. Only this time, those tools were aimed at a small rock riffle guarding the entrance to a deep backwater area littered with logs and stumps.

In preparation for the Illinois Bassmaster Invitational, Yelas had flown over both the Illinois and Mississippi rivers, searching for a place to escape the crowds. He knew that the better pools (like 26) had limited fishable water and would be congested once the tournament began. From the air, he noticed that the rear of the creek had clearer water than other areas.

Making the long run up the creek on the first practice day, the 2002 CITGO Bassmaster Classic presented by Busch champion was stymied by a stretch of solid rock covered by a 4-inch layer of

water. At that point, Yelas walked — rod and reel in hand — about three miles into the backwater area and proceeded to get about 20 strikes.

He returned to the shoal on the third practice day and never made a cast. Instead, he spent the entire day trying to dig a trench in solid rock and make enough room to float his Skeeter boat through. Finally, he surrendered all hopes of reaching this private fishing hole.

That night, Mother Nature did what Jay Yelas' hard work could not — it rained enough to put almost 3 feet of water above that riffle.

Predictably, the sudden influx of water ruined this backwater pond on the first day of competition. But by the final round, it had cleared and Yelas was able to catch one of the largest stringers of an extremely difficult tournament (8 pounds, 13 ounces) to jump from 47th to fourth place.

Yelas was not surprised. Once again, a backwater area had rewarded his perseverance to penetrate it.

"That pick-and-shovel thing was no big deal for me," says Yelas. "In the past, I've been able to shovel out the mouth of a sandbar or use a handsaw to cut my way through trees at the mouth of little hidden sloughs. Anything it takes to get back in there. In tournaments, you are always looking for something different, and one of the best things you can hope for is a backwater area that nobody is fishing.

"The part I like best about backwaters is that they don't get fished heavily by local fishermen either, because usually they are harder to get into at certain times of the year. When the water comes up just enough to let you get into these backwater spots, you have a virgin fishery."

Yelas is asked to define the term *backwater* area.

"Backwaters, to me, include the back end of a creek or a little shoot off of the rear of a creek or a small slough off of the main river," he replies. "These are places that are generally hard to get to. They are typically very shallow — 5 feet or less — but you will occasionally find a deep hole. Backwaters almost always have discolored water."

Backwater areas are normally located near the headwaters of river-fed impoundments, where the conditions more closely resemble a river than a reservoir. When most anglers speak of backwater areas, they think of the upper ends of impoundments of the Tennessee, Arkansas and Mississippi rivers, for example. The backwater sections of these reservoirs are narrow and serpentine — and loaded with submerged boating hazards.

Yelas probably has the most extensive backwater experience of any fisherman. Growing up in California, he learned at an early age the value of the more remote sections of the Western reservoirs. He later expanded that knowledge with a thorough education in the backwater areas of Eastern impoundments.

Pro Profile
JAY YELAS
Hometown: Tyler, Texas
Birthdate: 9-2-1965

BASS Career Highlights
Tournament Titles: 5 (2002 CITGO Bassmaster Classic, 2001 Missouri Invitational, 1997 Missouri Invitational, 1995 Bassmaster Superstars, 1993 Maryland Top 100 Pro Divison)
Times in the Classic: 12
Times in the Money: 115
Total Weight: 5,038 lbs.
Career Winnings: $1,118,632
Avg. Per Tournament: $6,392.18

In less than a decade Jay Yelas cashed into the BASS millionaire club of tournament winnings. His knack for discovering obscure techniques and patterns accounts for his success.

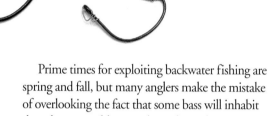

"When you think of the West, you think of the deep, canyon-type lakes, like Powell, Mead, Roosevelt and Mohave; lakes that don't have backwaters," Yelas explains. "But other lakes, like Havasu and Martinez, do have them. And I've won tournaments in those places.

"Backwaters in Western lakes are a little clearer," he says. "They require using finesse baits, whereas in the East we throw big spinnerbaits and jig-and-pigs. The backwater fishing in the West demands flipping little tubes and small jigs and throwing small spinnerbaits."

Prime times for exploiting backwater fishing are spring and fall, but many anglers make the mistake of overlooking the fact that some bass will inhabit those less-accessible areas throughout the year.

In spring, backwaters are at their most productive, supercharged by the spawning ritual that sends big female bass and their smaller male mates seeking the comfort of these sheltered sections.

In the weeks before the bedding takes place, Yelas looks for prespawn bass to be holding in the deepest water available in the backwater region.

"The easiest way to find these places is to look at the shoreline and see if there are any hills coming down that could signal some sort of steep underwater bank," he says. "If the shoreline is flat, usually the terrain

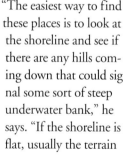

IN THE FALL, anglers will find bass in backwater areas. Yelas suggests keying on baitfish instead of cover when searching for fish.

under the water will be flat. But a steep bank generally indicates deep water, and right off of that steep bank is an ideal prespawn place. I slow roll a spinnerbait or fish a jig-and-pig along the steeper banks.

"Once the water starts to warm and the fish get closer to spawning, I look for stumps, cattails, bulrushes or tules, because those fish will get around shallower cover on flatter banks. Spawning time in the backwater areas means flipping with a tube jig, a lizard or small plastic crawfish. This is when you'll catch the biggest bass of the year in the backwaters."

Yelas emphasizes that line size doesn't change significantly from season to season in backwater situations. The natural cover (fallen trees, stumps, buckbrush and vegetation) demands heavy line, and the off-colored water allows you to get away with it.

For postspawn bass, Yelas returns to a spinnerbait, but drops to a smaller version (1/8- or 1/4-ounce with No. 2 and 3 Colorado blades) to better imitate small fry, shad and minnows that have recently hatched. He works it at a medium speed around any type of backwater cover adjacent to the spawning sites.

Summertime is probably the most underrated season for backwater fishing.

June through September brings some outstanding action on white buzzbaits, according to Yelas. This is fun fishing at its best, when a noisy buzzer brought past a stump or log in the shallowest of water is likely to produce a jarring strike, even on the hottest days of the year. In summer, Yelas also utilizes a 1/4-ounce spinnerbait and flips plastic crawfish, lizards and tube jigs.

"A large percentage of the fish will stay in the backwater areas throughout the summer," he adds, "but they sometimes will migrate out to the mouth of that area or adjacent to the river where they will stack up on a 50-yard stretch of bank.

"In the fall, the fish tend to move back into the backwaters and the key then is to look for the baitfish. If you find shad all the way in the back of the backwater area, that's where you need to be fishing. A lot of times in the fall, the bass don't relate

to cover as much as they do to the baitfish. Look for baitfish flipping on the surface, and fish those areas with shallow running crankbaits."

Winter is the least productive season in these backwater sloughs. Many of the bass will migrate out to the nearest creek or river channel, but a jig-and-pig or large spinnerbait fished methodically will occasionally produce a big bass in the interior of a backwater region. Yelas recommends targeting the deepest water and steepest banks available in these shallow areas.

Catching fish in these spots is the easy part. Getting into the backwaters is the challenge.

RESIDENT BACKWATER fish will sometimes concentrate at the mouth of a backwater area in summertime to take advantage of current and food.

STRUCTURE & COVER

Weeds and wood
are places where
the big bass hide . . .

LOOK FOR PATTERNS within patterns when fishing wood, such as a single tree extending past others growing in a group.

BASS IN THE WOODS
Look for wood cover no one else fishes

TUCKED AWAY near the end of a press release for a BASS tournament held on Georgia's Lake Lanier was a short quote from Denny Brauer explaining how he had caught 18 bass to finish third with 45 pounds, 14 ounces.

"A lot of the fish came from pieces of wood that you wouldn't expect fish to be around," he said.

Just what are "pieces of wood" and how does the Camdenton, Mo., pro probe them?

"Wood cover can take many different shapes, some of them obvious forms of cover and some of them things that the average angler overlooks," Brauer explains. "Among the obvious visible examples would be a laydown log, a boat dock or a 2-by-4 stuck in the mud with its tip above water.

"But many times those obvious examples of wood cover have subtle woody cover within their overall framework, or nearby. For example, at Lake Lanier I caught several nice bass from a dock that I

know many people had fished hard — and unsuccessfully — in the tournament."

The former Classic winner notes that most anglers worked the ladders, posts and ends of the docks. But with his polarized sunglasses, Brauer could see a dark shadow in shallow water under the walkway leading to the dock. That shadow turned out to be a stump, and it produced two crucial keepers. At a different dock, he enticed three keepers from a lamp post several yards from the structure.

"Parts of old trees are excellent pieces of wood. Many people will fish an old laydown that extends out from the shoreline. But on the downstream side, there may be some old branches, as well as debris stuck in those branches. Again, that's where the unpressured bass and the biggest bass in that area will likely be."

Brauer lists other examples of "invisible" wood as well. Sections of wood pilings that have been disengaged from the main piling, parts of a pier that have settled in a cove pocket, and the root system from such trees as cypress are all prime examples. He wears sunglasses to find this subsurface wood, and he suggests that a quality pair of sunglasses is necessary for putting together a wood-related pattern.

A pattern that revolves around pieces of wood can also involve more traditional fishing approaches. For instance, Brauer often keys on dead willow trees standing among live ones, or a single bush that extends farther out into the water than those around it, or perhaps a stickup on the lip of the main channel that borders a flat.

Other examples include twigs that indicate a crappie brushpile near a dock, a log that has become entangled among buckbush branches that extend out over the water, a "slick" tree with no bark standing among a cluster of other partially submerged trees with bark, an isolated tree "out in the middle of nowhere," and a host of other situations. In short, a major key is finding wood that is different in some respect from otherwise similar cover nearby.

LURES FOR WOOD

Wood accounts for bass throughout the year, and Brauer employs certain lures based on the seasonal habits of bass.

"In spring, you have a wide choice of lures for working wood," he says. "For isolated cover, such as a stump or a post, I'll use a jerkbait. For bass down in dense cover, I'll toss a soft jerkbait over the fish and try to draw them up.

"For cover at, near or around docks, I'll bump a medium running crankbait in a crawdad pattern against it. The same technique also works sometimes

Pro Profile
DENNY BRAUER

Hometown: Camdenton, Mo.
Birthdate: 2-3-1949

BASS Career Highlights
Tournament Titles: 13 (2002 Alabama Tour Pro, 1998 Maryland Top 150 Pro, 1998 Bassmaster Classic, 1988 North Carolina Top 100 Pro, 1998 Georgia Top 100 Pro, 1993 Bassmaster Superstars, 1993 Virginia Invitational, 1992 Bassmaster BP MegaBucks, 1990 Tennessee Top 100 Pro, 1987 Super Invitational, 1986 Texas Bassmaster Invitational, 1985 Chattanooga Invitational, 1984 Texas Invitational)
Times in the Classic: 17   **Times in the Money:** 134
Total Weight: 5,856 lbs., 6 ozs.   **Career Winnings:** $1,655,351.90
Avg. Per Tournament: $7,771.61

BASS millionaire tournament winner Denny Brauer is an expert at fishing wood, ranging from timber to brushpiles and boat docks.

Know Your Bait

One drawback to fishing wood is that strikes from bass you find there can be difficult to detect.

"Most people don't recognize bites many times," Denny Brauer says. For this all too common occurrence, how does a fisherman cope?

"In warmer water, you don't have much of a problem," he says. "But when using a jig in colder water, many people do have trouble detecting a hit. The solution is to try to visualize what the jig is doing underwater. In other words, have total awareness of your bait. Mentally picture what the jig does when it contacts the wood."

By simplifying lure choices and becoming comfortable with a particular rod, a fisherman becomes more aware of how a jig feels in a variety of cover and bottom situations. This "bait awareness" is crucial for feeling subtle jig strikes.

"Everyone wants to feel the bite. In jig fishing that doesn't happen. You have to anticipate the bite. It's almost a sixth sense," counsels Brauer.

"If you lose bait awareness, you jerk. If it feels too heavy or too light, jerk. If you think it should have hit bottom and it doesn't, jerk. It has to become automatic. The biggest fish I ever caught, I would have bet anyone a hundred dollars that it really wasn't a fish."

A JIG AND pork rind is Denny Brauer's first choice for fishing wood in cold water.

for laydowns or stumps. To work the tops of crappie brushpiles, nothing beats a stickbait — like the Zara Spook. And any time you have aggressive springtime fish around wood, always try a spinnerbait."

FISH INCONSPICUOUS FEATURES around the periphery of a boat dock, such as a single stickup planted by the owner.

Come summer, Brauer relies on bottom-bumping baits to reach fish that station themselves in greater depths. Baits such as plastic worms, crawfish and lizards excel at drawing out bass from stumps along creek channels, wood pilings in deep water out from the main piling, and limbs near sunken trees in deep, outside channel bends. To fetch the biggest bass from these deep water zones, this angler believes a deep running crankbait is many times the top choice.

Nevertheless, early and late during the warmwater period, bass will often move to shallow wood cover — such as stickups in coves, stumps on flats and shoreline brush. To take advantage of this shallow water daily migration, Brauer favors a buzzbait.

Bass typically move shallow sometime during fall, and Brauer believes that isolated wood really comes into its own then. Among key targets, he lists sticks of wood on mud flats, logs that have been partially silted in and rest in coves, and brushpiles that crappie fishermen have planted far out from the bank. Spinnerbaits cultivate strikes at this time, and a jig-and-pig does well.

For cold water, Brauer relies on basically one lure, his namesake jig.

"A Strike King Pro Model Jig is my first choice in cold water, regardless of whether I am pitching or

The Many Faces Of Jig Bites

For inexperienced jig fishermen, perhaps the biggest challenge is detecting strikes.

When it comes to these rubber skirted baits, few lures attract such a variety of strikes — from bone-jarring assaults to a nonaggressive mouthing from an inactive bass.

"You have to be willing to go out there and embarrass yourself," Denny Brauer advises. "You have to be willing to jerk, because with jig bites, for some reason they have the ability to inhale that bulky bait and exhale it without you knowing it.

"There are other times when they are aggressive, and you are going to see your line jump. That's when it's, 'Katie, bar the door!' You're going to see your line swim sideways and do different things. Hang on and set the hook.

"When you are fishing around targets and using the pitching and flipping technique, you just have to develop total lure awareness. What does your lure feel like? You are almost weighing it every time you go to pick up on it. And if I go to pick up real slow and subtle with the rod tip, and it feels like there is weight there — no matter how much weight — I'm probably going to drop that rod tip and set the hook. Because if you get into feeling contests, the only thing you are going to feel is that fish spitting that bait out."

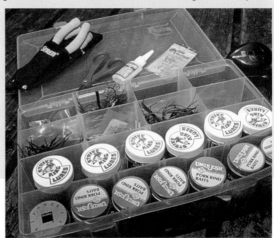

BASS WILL MOVE to shallow wood cover such as shoreline brush in summertime to ambush prey, says Denny Brauer.

flipping," he stresses. "For shallow targets and when I pitch, I choose the 3/8-ounce jig. For deeper targets and when I pitch or cast in clear water, I go with the 1/2-ounce model. For bigger bass, I add a large Uncle Josh pork frog to the jig.

"Also, the colder the water, the slower my retrieve is. And if I find an isolated piece of wood cover, I retrieve the bait into the cover and leave it there for a long time. Periodically, I will softly shake the jig and let the rattle do its thing. The goal is to antagonize a bass and get a reflex strike."

Regarding color combinations, for muddy water Brauer favors a black skirt with chartreuse strands and a black or black/chartreuse frog. For clear to stained water, he prefers a black skirt with blue flashes and black pork; and for strictly clear water the choice is a pumpkin/green pepper skirt with chocolate brown pork. A black or blue skirt performs well any time of year.

PORK IS MORE pliable, more fluid and more lifelike than plastic, according to Denny Brauer.

WOOD-FISHING LESSONS

Brauer strongly believes that learning how to fish pieces of wood can result in more and bigger bass. And he cites the 1992 Bassmaster Classic as a prime example.

"It was the last day of that Classic, and I needed a couple of fish to finish high," he recalls. "I pulled up to some old pieces of a wooden dock, caught three keepers, and finished second.

"Don't ever overlook a piece of wood. Although fishermen can argue about whether wood or grass is better, that really doesn't matter. Grass isn't found everywhere, so wood is the best form of cover you'll find in the majority of the waters."

PLASTIC FROGS can raise powerful strikes from bass buried in matted grass.

ATTACKING THE GRASS
How to find bass in a 'haystack'

THE PROBLEM WITH FISHING GRASS is that the water gets in the way. In these situations, what you can't see can hurt you. Instead of trying to read and fish a grassbed as if it were a section of shoreline structure with contours and irregularities to point out bass-holding areas, fishermen often find themselves meandering around the weeds.

For veteran Ohio BASS pro Joe Thomas, there is definitely nothing haphazard about it. Like shoreline structure, grass can be patterned and picked apart as deftly as a main lake point.

THE SEASONS

Of the factors critical to grass fishing success, the seasonal pattern is clearly No. 1. However, unlike the four part seasonal breakdown, the grass fishing year can be divided into three phases:

Phase 1: Early spring — With water temperatures lower than 60 degrees (usually in March and April), the grass is short and just beginning to emerge. With this wide-open situation, Thomas recommends working fast moving lures (lipless crankbaits, jerkbaits and crankbaits) over the top of the grass. If the fish are finicky, slow down with either a Texas rigged plastic worm (typically 3/16-ounce slip sinker or less) or a Carolina rigged lizard with a 1/2-ounce weight and at least a 3-foot leader to keep the bait above the grass.

Key search area: Heart of the grassbed or inner edge.

Phase 2: May/June — As the season progresses and the grass matures, fishermen

(Opposite page) BASS SEEK refuge from hot water in the shade provided by grass, making it a key spring and summer bass target.

Pro Profile
JOE THOMAS
Hometown: Milford, Ohio
Birthdate: 8-19-1961

BASS Career Highlights
Tournament Titles: Not yet won a Bassmaster title.
Times in the Classic: 4
Times in the Money: 75
Total Weight: 4,295 lbs., 1 oz.
Career Winnings: $314,948.47
Avg. Per Tournament: $1,598.72

Joe Thomas is a BASS touring pro whose expertise is in fishing grass of all types.

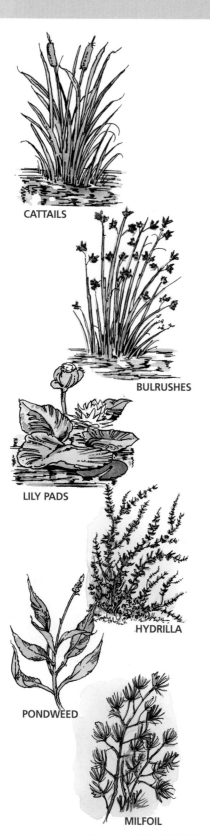

CATTAILS

BULRUSHES

LILY PADS

HYDRILLA

PONDWEED

MILFOIL

begin having difficulty working different lures over or through the grass. At this point, single-hook lures, such as spinnerbaits, are very effective at getting through midrange grass that is thicker, but not yet topped out. And, they serve as an equally powerful search tool. Topwater plugs (Zara Spook, Pop-R) and buzzbaits also become productive.

Key search area: The outer edge.

Phase 3: Summer through fall — The grass becomes mostly or completely topped out, which shifts the focus to one of three *key search areas*:

(1) On top — The lure choices become limited to topwater lures, such as surface frogs and poppers.

(2) Along the edges — As the grass tops out, the fish will move to the outer edges to ambush prey.

(3) Penetrating the grass — With grass 4 to 10 feet deep, it is often difficult to get bass to blow up through the canopy. Thomas uses either a 1/2- or 1-ounce Texas rigged plastic worm or crawfish imitator. Or, a 1-ounce, black/blue jig with a crawfish trailer.

FISHING THE EDGES

Whether fishing inside edges in the early spring or outside edges as the year progresses, finding irregularities along these grasslines is crucial to one's success.

"I key on any irregularity: a divot in the grass, a small notch that could signify a bottom contour or composition change, or a narrow gap where the current may flow through. The only time haphazard casting works is in the early spring, when you can fish fast moving baits over vast areas of grass. Even then, if a fisherman is paying attention, he will find that most of his bites come in a very specific depth range," counsels Thomas.

"In summer and fall, grass fish tend to congregate. When you catch one, you can drop a marker buoy (especially while fishing a jig through the grass) and catch five or six fish from an area no bigger than your boat."

Finding the edges — "When it's topped out, it's easy to see the edges. But earlier in the year or whenever the water level is above the mature grass, you need to rely on your bow-mounted electronics," says Thomas.

The best method to find these edges electronically is to zigzag the grassline. For example, if the grass is to your left and open water is to the right, kick your

REGARDLESS OF THE VARIETY, aquatic vegetation provides habitat for the entire food chain, from plankton and microscopic organisms to baitfish and bass.

trolling motor to the right until you hit clean water, then kick it to the left until you start detecting the grass. By repeating this zigzag movement, a fisherman can very precisely define the contour of the grass edge.

Defined edges — A grassbed that offers well-defined edges (especially in late summer and fall) provides a highway for bass. The edges also offer equally defined irregularities that make the fish finding process much easier.

"If you're facing a huge field of grass that tapers out to infinity, you really don't have a place to start. A defined grassline provides those 2- to 3-foot areas that you know will most likely hold some fish."

Structure considerations — Although the presence of structure, such as boulders and rockpiles, adjacent to grass can attract bass in northern waters, like Minnetonka or Thousand Islands, quite often the most important element is that grass does not grow in these locations. The same situation occurs in high or low spots where grass does not grow. In these zones, small rings or islands create a perimeter fringed with grass — something that provides productive ambush areas for bass.

Shade — "Early in the year, you're looking for a fertile situation, one where the grass provides refuge for baitfish and ambush areas for bass. Later in the year, when the grass tops out, shade becomes the No. 1 item for bass holding under the canopy," advises Thomas.

Grass types and water depth —While it is probably a mistake to categorize different grass types as good or bad, it is critical to know how much water exists under the canopy when fishing matted vegetation. If an area is choked with weeds (without some water depth beneath the canopy), it won't hold many fish. Bass need alleys to move through the grass.

LOOK FOR BASS holding in variations of the bottom contour when fishing bulrushes, which are found in natural lakes and treeless reservoirs of the Northeast.

LIPLESS crankbaits are a staple for pros who fish hydrilla-laden reservoirs. Most strikes occur when you rip the trebles free of the grassy snag.

IN SUMMERTIME, position the boat parallel to the edge of a dense hydrilla bed and pitch a heavy jig to the fish holding beneath the edge of the vegetation.

TECHNIQUES FOR FISHING ROCKPILES
Rocky cover offers year-round bass action

MIKE AUTEN'S KNOWLEDGE of the correct way to fish rockpiles first became known to the angling public when he finished third at a BASS tournament held a few years ago on Lake Minnetonka. At that Minnesota impoundment, the Kentucky pro excelled by probing rocks on the outside of weed edges.

Sounds simple, doesn't it? In truth, a great deal more goes into making Auten's rockpile strategy so successful. The first step is to determine just what traits a prime rockpile exhibits.

"A massive rockpile is, in effect, just a hump; with today's advanced electronics, plenty of anglers can locate a hump and fish it hard," says Auten. "A rockpile 20 to 25 yards long is too easy to find and can be overfished.

"The ideal size for a rockpile is about half the size of a bass boat. Many anglers will overlook one this size, and the individual who does take the time to find it will probably have the structure to himself. What's more, small rockpiles are very easy to work efficiently and quickly."

WHEN TO FISH ROCKPILES

Auten explains that rockpiles draw a number of bass forage species throughout spring, summer and fall. Crawfish especially are attracted to this form of cover during the year, and sculpins, minnows and various species of shad make regular appearances as well. From the algae that thrive on the rocks to the tiny, dark niches among the stones to the various forms of flotsam that settle on this cover, a rockpile is an integral part of the food chain.

Rockpiles begin to pulsate with life early in the spring. Crawfish emerge from their winter slumber, and prespawn bass congregate around this cover as they seek out the protein-rich crustacean.

After the spawn, bass naturally stop at rockpiles on their way to deep water. There they recuperate from reproduction by taking advantage of the buffet table this cover offers. During the autumn months, a rockpile continues to attract bass, as baitfish are drawn there.

WHERE TO FIND ROCKPILES

The vast majority of time, this BASS pro seeks out offshore rockpiles.

"If you pick up a lake map, you will probably see underwater channels, creek intersections, points, breaklines and various other changes in depth," he says. "Except for points, most of these

places will be found well away from the shoreline. A rockpile is really just a type of cover, and the best situation for a bass fisherman is to find cover on bottom structure. By structure, I mean a place where there is a change in the lake's bottom.

"I also feel that offshore rockpiles are more productive on lakes that lack quality shoreline cover and that receive a lot of fishing pressure. By necessity, the bass have to move away from the banks. On the other hand, a lake that offers great shoreline cover will rarely have rockpiles that produce big time. The fish simply do not have to move offshore to find food."

Rockpiles may come in many forms, he adds. In man-made lakes, old bridge pilings can be considered rockpiles, as can rock slides below bluffs,

Pro Profile
MIKE AUTEN
Hometown: Benton, Ky.
Birthdate: 8-6-1969

BASS Career Highlights
Tournament Titles: Has not yet won a Bassmaster title.
Times in the Classic: 3
Times in the Money: 43
Total Weight: 2,864 lbs., 13 ozs.
Career Winnings: $212,716.67
Avg. Per Tournament: $1,599.37

Mike Auten prides himself on being highly skilled at patterning bass in rockpiles, one of the most inconspicuous but highly productive types of bass cover.

Rocky Lure Choices

The same lures that catch bass in weeds and wood work well around rocks, but there are some differences, says Texas BASS pro Jay Yelas.

"One of the biggest advantages to fishing rocky areas is you can use a lure with an exposed hook, which is going to improve your catch ratio," he explains. "You'll still get snagged, but usually that's because the lure has caught in the cracks of the rocks, and that will happen with or without the hook exposed."

Yelas says that bass relate to the shady side of rockpiles, so he chooses lures that fall vertically or spiral on the drop, like jigs, grubs, soft jerkbaits and tube baits. Bright days call for pinpoint casting because the strike zone is very specific, even in deep water. Also, a double-tail spider jig, rigged on a 3/8-ounce leadhead, can be fished on the fall or swum over the cover. Simply wind it slowly over the bottom, occasionally allowing it to bounce off the rocks. That's a big fish tactic for summertime.

and stone that was blasted out in the building of now-submerged roadbeds. On tidal rivers, some of Auten's best fishing has taken place where ships dumped their ballast. And on Kentucky Lake, his home water, one of his favorite locales is a place where a landowner piled broken bricks and cinder blocks.

Interestingly, Auten adds that while many fishermen like to sink small trees and brush on bottom structure, he likes to do the same with rocks on Kentucky Lake. Over the years, he has been able to put together quite a "milk run" by doing so.

HOW TO FISH ROCKPILES

For the prespawn period, Mike Auten's No. 1 option is a flat-sided crankbait, which exhibits a wide wobble at slow retrieves. Many fat crankbaits have to be retrieved too quickly to wobble erratically, thus making them ineffective for coldwater bass that might not be prone to chase down a fast moving artificial bait.

The Kentuckian also tries to make his crankbaits deflect off the base, sides, or tip of a rockpile in order to elicit reflex strikes. Any cast (and this holds true throughout the year) should be made "upstream" so that the bait returns with the current, and with the boat positioned in water deeper than the cover.

Another prespawn reliable is a Carolina rig. Among the essential components is an egg sinker (which does not hang up in the stones as readily as a bullet sinker does), a 2-foot-long leader and a 4- or 6-inch lizard.

A final lure is a 3/4- or 1-ounce spinnerbait. His favorite model for clear water has

A FLAT-SIDED crankbait fished around the periphery of an isolated rockpile is Mike Auten's first choice for fishing rocky cover in the prespawn.

tandem blades, and he fishes it by slow rolling over and around the rocks.

The postspawn period is Auten's favorite time to probe rockpiles.

"A rockpile that sits on the first breakline out from a spawning flat can be an awesome place then," he says. "You might have to check three or four places before you find any fish, but when you do catch one, you often can quickly catch a limit.

"A flat-sided crankbait is still an awesome tool, just select color patterns that match those of the baitfish on your home lake. Fat crankbaits also now come into their own, especially if you want to give the fish a different look."

The pro adds that Carolina rigged lizards continue to produce, but in warmer weather he turns to a jig-and-pig instead of a spinnerbait as his third option. The pro pairs the bait with a 6 1/2-foot medium-heavy baitcaster and 12-pound-test line.

But Auten does not practice standard cast-and-retrieve for jigs. Once the bait touches down on the rubble, he holds his rod tip at the 10 o'clock position, then snaps the rod up and back as if he were setting the hook.

The pro maintains what he calls a "slightly slack" line as the bait falls. As soon as it contacts the bottom, he "pops" the lure again in the same manner. If the line twitches or feels heavy — and Auten says line

watching is a must — he quickly sets the hook.

Georgia BASS pro Mickey Bruce receives credit for popularizing this technique, and Auten says it works well for bass, whether they are holding right on top of a pile or suspending off to the side. He also emphasizes that rods longer than 6 1/2 feet should not be utilized because they pull the jig too far away from the cover during the popping process.

Come autumn, fat crankbaits in shad patterns move to the forefront, and lipless crankbaits and spinnerbaits are also quite effective. But one of the best ways to entice rockpile bass then is with a topwater lure.

On largemouth lakes that become clear in the fall, as well as in smallmouth hot spots such as New York's famous Thousand Islands region, surface lures, such as poppers and stickbaits can draw fish up from rockpiles. Jerkbaits, including the soft plastic variety, are similarly efficient ways to catch fish.

The small, isolated rockpiles that Mike Auten prefers to visit are among his favorite forms of cover across the country.

"A rockpile can be a wonderful place to fish throughout much of the year, regardless of its depth, the water clarity or whether largemouth or smallmouth predominate in the lake or river," he says. "If you are in tune with your electronics, you can put together a rockpile game plan that is so subtle, even people who are watching you fish will not know what you are doing."

CAROLINA RIGGED plastics and leadhead baits are productive in the prespawn when fish suspend above rockpiles.

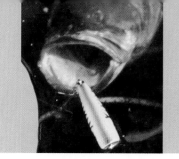

REACTION BITE lures like a popper will attract distant fish cruising bare banks in search of a meal.

FIND BASS ON BARE BANKS
Don't overlook featureless shorelines

BARE BANKS COULD RIGHTFULLY be called the "Cinderella structure" of bass fishing.

Remember, Cinderella was a plain-Jane who swept floors and gathered leftovers behind her more flamboyant stepsisters. But with the wave of a wand, she became the belle of the ball, a moth that turned into a beautiful butterfly.

What's the connection to bare banks and structure fishing? Simple. Bare banks are plain-Janes in their own right — no sexy dropoffs or tantalizing timber tops or rockpiles. Compared to sunken channels, points, roadbeds, etc., they are as blasé as a chambermaid. Most anglers ignore bare banks in favor of more alluring structure.

However, despite their appearance, many bare banks are beauties when it comes to producing bass. Sometimes the dullest-looking shorelines attract big schools of fish. Couple this with the lack of pressure on these spots, and the combination can yield fairy tale catches for anglers who wave their casting wands over the right bare banks at the right times.

BASS pro Mark Davis is recognized in the bass fishing world as one of the sport's most versatile anglers. And "Cinderella" banks, often overlooked by many skilled anglers, are a big reason why Davis has been so successful in his pro career, which includes a world championship title.

"I tell you, bare banks can be good fishing spots — not all of them, but some of them," Davis notes. "Also, they're ignored by most people. So the pressure in other areas of the lake causes fish to shift to where they aren't pounded, and a lot of

(Opposite page)
MARK DAVIS reached the pinnacle of competitive bass fishing probing barren banks often ignored by his peers.

Pro Profile
MARK DAVIS
Hometown: Mt. Ida, Ark.
Birthdate: 10-11-1963

BASS Career Highlights
Tournament Titles: 1 (1995 Bassmaster Classic)
Times in the Classic: 11
Times in the Money: 102
Total Weight: 4,484 lbs., 2 ozs.
Career Winnings: $773,371.30
Avg. Per Tournament: $4,863.97

In 1995, Davis became the first pro ever to win Angler of the Year and the Classic in the same season. His Classic victory on High Rock Lake in Greensboro, N.C., was due primarily to his prowess with a crankbait, solidifying his reputation as one of the Tour's elite crankbait fishermen.

times this means bare banks. This is why I pay these nothing-looking banks a lot of attention, and I catch fish off them that most other anglers don't know are there."

Bass use these places despite the lack of obvious features. And because there aren't many features, the ones that are there have the potential to draw in a lot of fish. These places can be real "sleepers."

THE ONLY WAY to learn which bare banks are productive is to test them out, says Mark Davis.

OVERVIEW OF BARE BANKS

Bare banks exist in virtually all reservoirs and lakes in the country. They are void stretches of clay, sand, mud or gravel or composites of these materials. Bare banks may border creek embayments, main river channels or islands.

HIDDEN BENEATH the watery surface of a bare bank can be found plenty of bass habitats: rock, wood, brush, contour changes.

BASS STRUCTURE may be just yards away from the expansive bare banks found in Western reservoirs.

Some run for short distances; others stretch for hundreds of yards. Still, the thread that ties all bare banks together is their lack of obvious features.

The degree to which bass use bare banks varies from lake to lake and even from one bank to the next. Bare banks in deeper and/or older lakes tend to attract more fish than do similar banks in shallower, newer lakes. The latter waters usually have other, higher quality structure to draw the fish. "Bare banks aren't as important in lakes that have timber or grass or lots of up-and-down bottom structure," says Davis.

He adds, however, that even in lakes with plenty of other structure, some bare banks still hold bass, and these can be honey holes because they are rarely fished.

"The only way to learn which banks are good is to test-fish them," he says. "This takes a lot of time, and this is why fishing bare banks is more practical for anglers on their home lakes than for pros that move around from one lake to the next."

The word "wind" rings Davis' bell when he considers bare banks. "Wind is one of the main keys," he emphasizes. "Fishing along a bare bank is 100 times better if there's a wind blowing onto it, especially on a clear lake. The waves 'blow in' baitfish. They stir up the bottom and expose crawfish. They break up sunlight penetration. Overall, wind blowing on a bare bank creates prime feeding conditions, and it causes the bass to be shallower and more active."

One other note about bare banks: They hold an extra attraction to smallmouth and spotted bass. Davis says that if a lake holds these two species, bare banks take on added importance. "If a lake only has largemouth, plain banks will be good sometimes. But if spots and smallmouth are present, they can be great virtually any time."

BASS LOCATIONS ALONG BANKS

Actually, the term "bare banks" contradicts the actual makeup of these void-looking structures.

"I don't think there's really such a thing as a bare bank," Davis says. "A bank may look bare if you're running down the lake at 50 miles per hour. But if you stop and really

PRESPAWN and spawning bass are drawn to the flash of a spinnerbait when it's slow rolled down a bare bank.

study and fish it, there's almost always something that will attract bass. It's just a matter of knowing what to look for and how to find it."

Davis finds bass near subtle changes or isolated features along bare banks. Examples include where a bank's makeup changes (i.e., gravel gives way to clay), where a creek channel swings near the bank, where a bank becomes flatter or steeper, or where a bank makes a slow turn. Also, underwater features along a bank are like beacons that draw bass. A stump, log or large rock can have a magnetic effect on fish swimming alongshore.

Knowing what to look for along bare banks and being able to find these spots are two different matters. A visual check is simple enough. An angler can see bank composition changes, shoreline turns or dark shadows of underwater stumps or logs. He can also study a topo map to find where channels angle near the bank. However, most fish-attracting features along bare banks are hidden from view and not shown on maps. Fishermen have two methods for finding them: electronic inspection with a depthfinder; and test-fishing.

Davis uses the simple approach: "I start on one end and fish it all," he says. "I feel like that's the only way I can really cover it effectively. I just decide to invest the time to go down it and check different areas and depths. That way I can do a thorough job of eliminating things and developing a reliable pattern."

As he fishes, Davis constantly monitors his bow-mounted depthfinder for objects or changes in the bank's contour.

"I like to find little shelves or places where the first break occurs closer to the shore," he says. "Again, these are the subtle little changes where bass are more likely to be. I feel that the only way I can find these places is by fishing the whole bank."

BAITS FOR BARE BANKS

For fishing bare banks, Davis relies on a small selection of dependable lures: crankbaits, spinnerbaits, jerkbaits, topwaters, grubs, jigs and plastic worms. Davis' lure selection and presentation (casting angle and method of retrieve) are influenced by the time of year and activity level of the bass.

Diving crankbaits are top choices for prospecting along bare banks from early spring through fall. Davis likes these baits because they can cover water quickly. Also, they can be cast right to the waterline, then bumped back down the bank's subsurface slope. This facilitates a check of depths ranging from a few inches to deeper than 10 feet.

He prefers a small, deep running bait in a crawfish pattern for the prespawn period, believing that bass will hit a smaller crankbait better than a bigger one.

SHALLOW RUNNING crankbaits are Mark Davis' top choice for finding prespawn bass cruising bare banks.

Another good bait for searching bare banks in early spring is a jerkbait. "Fishing a jerkbait is a good way to catch suspended bass. It's especially effective when the water first starts warming up (low to mid-40s). Also, I think jerkbaits are better in clear water than in dingy water," Davis adds.

When fishing this bait, Davis moves along the bank, making 45 degree casts to the shoreline. "I cast right to the water's edge, and I crank the bait four or five times to start it down, then I begin what I call a '1-2 retrieve'. I jerk, pause, jerk-jerk. I repeat this all the way back to the boat. Jerk, pause, jerk it twice. The colder the water, the slower I work the bait. Also, if the bank has a shallow slope, I use a jerkbait with a smaller lip. But if the bank has a steep slope, I use a spoonbill model with a bigger lip to make it dive deeper."

A spinnerbait is a third option for prospecting along bare banks in the prespawn and spawning periods. A spinnerbait should be cast shallow, then pulled down the slope with a middepth retrieve. Many times, if bass are actively feeding, they will be drawn in by the flash and vibration, and they will hit from below or beside the bait.

Davis alternates among crankbaits, jerkbaits and spinnerbaits to see which one the bass prefer on a given day.

"This is just a matter of trial and error," Davis notes. "One day the fish will hug bottom, and the diving crankbait works best. The next day they may be suspended, and the jerkbait is best. And the third day they might be roaming and feeding, and the spinnerbait is the trick. You just have to analyze the weather and water conditions and try to figure out how active the bass are and whether they're shallow, deep or suspended. Then pick the bait that will work best under those conditions. But if that bait doesn't work, try the other two types. Sometimes bass are hard to second-guess."

Davis says topwater baits fished along bare banks early and late in the day are a good pattern for heat-of-summer fishing. "I use a popper or stickbait, and I make long casts down the banks.

Covering Bare Banks

Fishing for bass in a maze of cover can be like finding the proverbial needle in a haystack. An unfished, isolated piece of cover on a bare bank is more like finding a single needle sticking out of a pin cushion. Californian Dean Rojas, a regular on the Bassmaster Tournament Trail, is well aware of this fact.

"I love running nothing banks, because nobody fishes them," says Rojas. "I just put the electric motor on high and cover a lot of water. Usually I'll stumble across a log or a stump under the water that you can't see when you're driving by. That's where you're going to catch a 4- or 5-pounder."

When running bare banks during practice rounds, Rojas quickly fishes them with a buzzbait or spinnerbait that has the hook covered to prevent hooking the bass. With these lures he can usually see the strike and judge the size of the bass without catching it.

Frequently, Rojas' bare bank reconnaissance turns up grassbeds just beneath the surface that hold good numbers of bass, especially when fishing clear, western impoundments. He typically finds the grass 2 to 10 feet deep from May through November.

"I don't know the name of the grass," says Rojas. "I call it 'sissy grass' because it's stringy and doesn't have a lot of mass or bulk. It's been out here in the West four or five years and is in most major reservoir chains now. It usually grows on sandy bottoms and really blooms up nicely in the summer."

Grass growing in front of a bare bank gave Rojas his first tournament victory. He was fishing an open event on Lake Havasu in August 1996. He fished the grass by working spinnerbaits, Zara Spooks and Pop-Rs over the greenery. The hot weather bass responded well to an upbeat pace and rewarded Rojas with a total weight of 24 pounds for the two day event, a respectable catch for Havasu and a bank that looked devoid of bass cover.

"The bass that feed in those grassbeds are usually here today and gone tomorrow," says Rojas. "I think it's because the shad are constantly moving in and out of the cover. But if you fish the grass at the right time, you can load the boat with bass."

This isn't the most consistent pattern in the world, but sometimes it will produce some big fish."

He also likes lipless crankbaits along bare banks when circumstances warrant, especially along flatter banks and where bass are chasing shad up close to shore, which happens often in early fall. Look for baitfish skipping out of the water, he recommends.

All in all, despite their "nonstructure" appearance, bare banks are a viable alternative for finding and catching bass. "I don't know if I'd rate bare banks as very important, but they can be good for all the reasons mentioned," Davis states. "There again, I think the biggest reason is because they're so overlooked by most fishermen." And that makes bare banks a spot worth checking.

RIGGING FOR BASS ON OFFSHORE STRUCTURE

Shun the shallows and strike paydirt in hidden hot spots

BY THEIR VERY NATURE, most Florida bass anglers are creatures of shallow water habit. They simply prefer to target shallow, visible cover — the easiest fishing of all.

Pete Thliveros is hardly the typical Florida fisherman. The Jacksonville native has developed a talent for locating and fishing unseen offshore structure, an ability that made him a top guide on the St. Johns River as well as one of the most successful pros on the CITGO Bassmaster Tour presented by Busch. He will tell you that this expertise is directly responsible for his appearances in the prestigious CITGO Bassmaster Classic presented by Busch and back-to-back gold medals in the bass fishing competition at the ESPN Great Outdoor Games.

It is a talent born out of necessity and frustration.

"I started fishing offshore in Florida because I got tired of pounding the shorelines behind everybody else," Thliveros says. "So I decided that there had to be more fish in open water and around offshore structure than there were along the banks. I forced myself to learn to fish offshore and look for irregular features on the bottom, different types of grass and subtle grasslines, brushpiles and shellbeds."

Thliveros learned on his own by spending countless hours probing the offshore portions of Lake Sante Fe near Gainesville, one of the clearest and deepest lakes in the state. He then applied what he had learned to the deeper, tidal-influenced structure in the St. Johns River, as well as lakes and reservoirs around the country.

"I'm more of an open water fisherman than a deep water fisherman," he adds. "Deep, to me, is 20 feet, which is probably the deepest I will catch fish. Some people catch fish from 20 to 40 feet, but I like to concentrate on 4 to 10 feet. That seems to be the most productive range for me in most lakes.

"Open water fishing involves going out and finding new places to fish. The most productive way I have of finding these places is driving along in my boat and watching my depthfinder constantly. Most of the time in practice for a tournament, I will drive from place to place while watching my depthfinder. If I see some sort of irregular feature or drop or shallow spot, I'll stop and fish it. These places are overlooked because most people go from Point A to Point B at 60

miles an hour. They go right over the fish. I drive 30 to 40 miles an hour in practice everywhere I go, and try to be real observant of the depthfinder and the lake itself."

When it comes to offshore structure, that depth range is largely new territory among Florida fishermen, and it's the least-explored water in other states.

"These places are overlooked because they may be out in the center of a bay and are hard to find," Thliveros explains. "Even if they see these places, most fishermen don't realize what the possibilities are — what's really there or how many fish may be nearby.

"Finding structure in natural lakes like we have in Florida is a lot harder than it is to find structure

Pro Profile
PETER THLIVEROS
Hometown: Jacksonville, Fla.
Birthdate: 4-7-1960

BASS Career Highlights
Tournament Titles: 3 (1997 Virginia Top 100 Pro, 1994 North Carolina Top 100 Pro Division, 1992 Florida Top 100 Pro Division)
Times in the Classic: 8
Times in the Money: 82
Total Weight: 4,036 lbs., 2 ozs.
Career Winnings: $617,929
Avg. Per Tournament: $3,961.08

Peter Thilveros developed his offshore angling skills in the highly pressured waters of Florida. He's applied his skills across the country to excel at his game.

Fishing Structure In Current

Learning to fish deep or offshore structure in a lake takes considerable time and effort. But being able to fish this submerged structure in current-laden waters — particularly tidal rivers — is a special talent, indeed.

"Knowing how to fish deep water lets me fish for the most underutilized fish in a river," says BASS pro Peter Thliveros, who grew up fishing portions of Florida's tidal-influenced St. Johns River that are largely ignored. "Very few people take the time to fish deep water, particularly in tidal rivers. The tide complicates matters.

"Learning to fish deep on a tidal river is a process of trial-and-error to find the right spots and then to figure out which tide the fish use to feed in that particular area. The tidal influence varies from place to place, and you have to learn that from experience.

"The first thing you should do if you happen to find a spot — like a main river dropoff where the fish are feeding — is take note of that tidal stage. Then go back and check the area occasionally. If the fish stop feeding when the tide changes, then you can pinpoint the particular tide stage in which the fish are most active."

For catching bass in these moving water situations, Thliveros utilizes three lures: a Texas rig 6- or 7-inch worm with a 1/4- to 3/8-ounce bullet weight on 12- to 14-pound-test line; a Carolina rig 4-inch worm on a 2- to 4-foot leader; and a Bomber 7A crankbait on 14-pound line.

"Boat positioning is critical with this type of fishing," he explains, "because certain areas require pinpoint casting. Positioning is dictated by the current. In some places you have to put the boat right against the bank and cast out — just to get out of the current. In others, you should sit in the current and cast in.

"The current makes this type of fishing a whole different ball game from deep structure fishing in calmer water. You have to know exactly where to cast, where the bait is going to go, where the fish are positioned and how fast the lure is going to move toward that spot."

OFFSHORE STRUCTURE can be the only place to catch bass during winter when the fish school on humps or channel ledges.

in a reservoir. First, there are no maps to show you where these spots might be located, so you have to use your depthfinder and your tackle and knowledge to find them. Natural structure in a Florida lake can be musselbeds, underwater grassbeds that aren't visible, or a real subtle change in the water depth. A 2-foot drop can be critical in a natural lake."

In reservoirs throughout the country, these changes are much more dramatic, making Thliveros' strategies even more productive.

Consider these three examples of the types of offshore structure situations Thliveros likes to find:

• In a tournament on Tennessee's Fort Loudon Reservoir, the pro was examining the underwater landmarks of a large bay that features several roadbeds, humps and dropoffs — all well-marked on maps. While idling over the 12-foot-deep flat out in the bay, he detected a drop to 15 feet — which automatically drew his attention. The depthfinder also indicated some type of structure was present. Closer inspection showed it to be a rockpile of about 40 feet by 20 feet, located about 100 yards from a creek channel.

His first cast of a Carolina rigged 4-inch worm onto the rockpile, brought in a bass of about 8 pounds. He went on to catch a limit of bass on that overlooked spot.

• In a May tournament on South Carolina's Lake Murray, most of the tournament field had settled on casting floating worms along the shoreline. Instead of following the crowd, Thliv-

A CAROLINA RIG can be used as a locator bait for covering offshore structure.

eros concentrated on looking for offshore structure and cover in the 5- to 12-foot range — the depth over which most other anglers were positioning their boats to work the bank. Thliveros managed to limit out each day by fishing isolated stumps or the first submerged grassline or breakline away from the shore.

The most productive spot he found consisted of two stumps about a boat-length apart on a subtle point. It surrendered five bass, including three in the 5- to 6-pound class.

• Thliveros was idling offshore in 10 to 12 feet of water in North Carolina's Lake Norman when he found a small rockpile located on a dip in the bottom contour that created a depth of 15 feet. His first bass weighed 7 pounds and the spot yielded several more keepers.

CRUISING OVER the top of expansive offshore flats can yield irregular features that hold quantities of bass overlooked by other anglers, says Peter Thliveros.

Thliveros is also a diehard flasher fan. He prefers a flasher because he says it provides a more instantaneous picture of the bottom and doesn't require the lingering attention needed to interpret a liquid-crystal unit.

Besides, Thliveros' main depthfinder is actually a Carolina rigged lure. After tossing out a marker buoy, he utilizes the heavy weight of the Carolina rig to map out the bottom structure, and then he fine-tunes his pattern by selecting the proper lure — which is based on the cover/structure as well as the aggressiveness of the bass.

"With any depthfinder, the cone angle of the transducer is so narrow that you can easily miss

Deep water debris can be a bass magnet. Once you fine a spot like this, fish it with a Carolina rig or crankbait from every possible angle.

a 2-foot drop in 10 feet of water," Thliveros emphasizes. "By dragging my Carolina rig along the bottom, I'm like a blind man with a cane. That weight tells me everything about the bottom — if it is a hard bottom, soft bottom, shell, rocks, stumps or grass. It identifies cover like nothing I've ever used. And it catches fish, because it provides a subtle presentation of the bait."

For fishing a Carolina rigged plastic, Thliveros most often uses a 7-foot medium-heavy rod, which features a fairly limber tip, and a high speed baitcasting reel, which is important for quickly removing any slack line before setting the hook on a Carolina rig. In clear water situations like Florida's Lake Sante Fe, he switches to lighter line and a 6 1/2-foot spinning outfit.

WHEN BASS are particularly aggressive, Thliveros goes after them with a deep diving crankbait. He matches the running depth of the bait with the depth of the structure.

His Carolina rig consists of a 1-ounce bullet weight, glass bead and small swivel on the 14- to 20-pound-test line. The leader usually ranges from 4 to 7 feet in length (based on the height of the structure or cover) and is made with 14- to 20-pound clear line.

A 6-inch melon-pepper or green-pumpkinseed lizard is his favorite Carolina rig bait for exploring offshore structure. "The reason the lizard is such a popular Carolina rig choice is because it combines a big bait with a subtle presentation," Thliveros says. "It is a big, bulky bait that has a lot of action and movement."

His other Carolina rig choices include: a shad-colored French fry lure — a straight piece of plastic with no built-in action — which resembles a Do-Nothing Worm without the hooks (it is especially good for finicky bass); a 5-inch grasshopper-colored ringworm; a 6-inch ribbon-tail worm; and a 4-inch finesse worm.

"With the Carolina rig, I use two basic retrieves," Thliveros adds. "One is a very slow, steady drag with the rod tip. The other is a slow, steady drag with intermittent jerks, fast pulls or erratic motions. When I get into an area where I feel a lot of stumps or shells, I pause it a lot and shake it in one spot until the fish come and get it. I let the fish tell me what kind of retrieve to use."

When the bass are especially aggressive, Thliveros' primary weapon is a crankbait. He matches his lures' diving depths to the depth of the structure, and he relies heavily on chartreuse, green, brown, firetiger and shad hues.

Thliveros occasionally fishes a big (3/4- to 1-ounce) spinnerbait, jig or Texas rigged worm. But, generally, the Carolina approach or crank-

A CAROLINA RIG and electronic flasher are two basic tools needed to find offshore bass structure.

ing will score best in these out-of-the-way bass hideouts.

"If more people would just move away from the bank and take the time to learn to fish a Carolina rig, it would open up a whole new world to them," Thliveros advises. "It certainly has for me."

EXPLORING AMBUSH POINTS
Try David Fritts' sweet spots for cranking

ASK ANY PROFESSIONAL about crankbait technique and eventually, somewhere in the conversation, he will mention David Fritts. To them, and to anyone who is a follower of the BASS circuit, Fritts is the undisputed master of the technique.

While there are many reasons for his dominance in crankbaiting, one of the most crucial factors is in his uncompromising attention to detail. Instead of being satisfied with choosing a productive lure, he wants to choose the *most* productive lure. The same applies in his approach to structure fishing.

For most fishermen, simply finding an area that holds fish is the goal. Once achieved, the refinement process doesn't go much further. Not with Mr. Fritts. To him, every piece of structure — points, flats, ridges, humps, etc. — offers one spot where most of the fish come to feed. Some call it the "sweet spot," but Fritts prefers to label these often small spots within spots, "ambush points."

Since every structure situation is as unique as a fingerprint, there is no set formula for finding the ambush point. There are, however, some useful guidelines.

First, an ambush point will most likely involve some sort of irregularity on the structure. This can be any number of things from a high spot, abrupt depth change, isolated cover or rock, anything that will collect both bait and bass. Unfortunately, these ambush points are not usually obvious, even with the help of sonar. In most cases, they're a subtle blend of things that don't immediately say, "Fish here."

Sonar can get you close though, offers Fritts, since ambush points are usually positioned where the shallowest water on the structure meets the deepest water. Find that transition, and somewhere in the immediate vicinity will be the best place on the entire structure to present your crankbait.

Second, while the general location of an ambush

Pro Profile
DAVID FRITTS
Hometown: Lexington, N.C.
Birthdate: 12-29-1956

BASS Career Highlights
Tournament Titles: 5 (1996 Minnesota Top 100 Pro, 1994 Georgia Top 100 Pro Division, 1993 Virginia Invitational, 1993 Bassmaster Classic, 1990 Virginia Top 100 Pro)
Times in the Classic: 6
Times in the Money: 69
Total Weight: 3,704 lbs., 2 ozs.
Career Winnings: $824,805
Avg. Per Tournament: $5,976.85

A world championship title and several BASS tour titles prove David Fritts has redefined crankbait fishing, making it more than just a mundane cast-and-retrieve technique.

Ambush Spots In The Prespawn

Bass use secondary points as a primary reference marker between the main lake and the backs of the creeks, pockets or flats where they spawn in the shallows.

As the water temperature climbs toward the mid-60s, bass begin to move deeper into creeks until they reach secondary points, which are their staging areas for the final leg of the migration into shallow spawning coves. Smaller male fish lead the way to the secondary points, while the bigger females linger behind on the primary points or deeper secondary points in the vicinity of the creek mouth.

"When the water temperature gets up around 61 or 62 degrees, I'll still fish the primary points, but I'll fish shallower, usually in around 5 to 12 feet of water," says Georgia pro Tom Mann Jr. "I rely more on crankbaits than jigs at this time, and I'll also start trying plastic worms. If I don't contact any bass on the primary points, I'll start working my way into the creek, fishing the secondary points until I locate the bass."

Visible substructure frequently concentrates bass on secondary points during the prespawn. Pay particular attention to fallen trees, stumps, logs, brush and any other likely cover objects.

point can be discovered with sonar, the exact position can only be determined by swimming a crankbait through it. As a result, a fisherman must know precisely how deep a particular lure will dive and how fast it reaches that maximum depth range.

By understanding that every crankbait follows a downward curving path like a pendulum, an angler can judge how far to cast beyond a target to make this arc intersect precisely with the ambush point.

In most instances, the object is to have the crankbait barely tick the structure as it wobbles past. It's a sometimes tricky maneuver to learn, since the lure is only at that depth for a brief period during the retrieve, and the ambush point may only measure in yards, if not feet. Of course, the payoff is a level of consistency in generating strikes that most casual crankbaiters might find astonishing.

Since many of these structure areas are located offshore, it is crucial that an angler know precisely where to position the boat to make productive casts. Although Fritts prefers not to use marker buoys, it's really a matter of personal preference how someone keeps track of his/her position — whether that means triangulating with shoreline features or dropping buoys.

THE GENERAL location of an ambush point can be found with sonar but a crankbait must be used to pinpoint the fish, says David Fritts.

Third, the process doesn't end with the successful discovery of an ambush point and making a cast that places the lure in this all-important strike zone. At this point, Fritts begins exploring different casting angles, trying to find the optimum path. While maximizing the potential of any spot is at the heart of Fritts' "ambush point" philosophy, there is a more basic reason, one that directly applies to weekend fishermen as much as professionals.

"By knowing the ambush points, I don't have to spend time going all the way around a point or all the way down a flat. I know exactly where to go and where to throw my bait. And, I know if the fish are biting right now — or not."

AN ASSORTMENT of crankbaits designed to run shallow, midrange and deep are required to work the varying depths of ambush points.

IRREGULARITIES IN bottom contour define ambush points. Sweet spots hold wood or rock positioned where the shallowest water meets a dropoff. A crankbait is the best tool for quickly finding such bass magnets.

SIMPLIFYING SONAR
Mastering a depthfinder begins at the ramp

A S SONAR UNITS have become increasingly more powerful and sophisticated, the demands upon bass fishermen also have grown. Not so much in absorbing every facet of this new technology or in understanding each feature, but in knowing what to use and what to leave behind.

This simplification process is at the very heart of what veteran Western pro Don Iovino has been preaching for nearly two decades.

"Sonar is your underwater eye. If you learn to interpret sonar — and so many anglers really can't interpret what they see — the results will be very satisfying," insists Iovino.

"A part of this misinterpretation is the result of fishermen not spending enough time looking at the sonar screen. They want sonar to be a magic bullet that will solve all their problems. They try to shorten the learning curve, but in many cases, they become a slave to the technology, not the master of it."

Yet another reason for misinterpreting the blips and lines painted by sonar pixels is the marketing methods used by the manufacturers themselves. In an attempt to show how sonar illustrates various angling situations, simulated screens often depict idealized versions of structure, cover and fish, notes Iovino. Unfortunately, these perfect illustrations sometimes show things that don't exist in the real world

At other times they show the exception and not the rule. Of these, the stylized fish "arcs" seen in advertisements can be reproduced on the water. That is, if the boat and fish are headed in the same direction, the cone angle passes over the bass uniformly and the fish is not exiting or entering the cone angle. Otherwise, fish can be illustrated by any number of slanted lines or abbreviated slashes, marks that may look more like underwater punctuation than anything remotely resembling an "arc."

For this reason and because bass echoes may be masked by surface clutter or submerged cover, Iovino and other professional anglers don't always rely on seeing fish to evaluate an area. If they do see a well-defined fish arc, that's a bonus.

The process of finding bass with sonar should be focused instead on evaluating the underwater environment and recognizing the keys that can lead you to fish. Even for sonar experts, this analysis always starts at the launch ramp.

From the very beginning, a canon of the Iovino sonar doctrine has been this: The marina area of any lake will always provide the most information first thing in the morning.

The launch ramp is the best place to set and assess the gray line setting. Since gray line gauges bottom hardness, and since launch ramps are invariably placed in areas with relatively hard bottoms, an angler knows what to expect from the gray line reading. A wider band on the sonar screen indicates a hard bottom, while a soft or mucky bottom, which absorbs more of the signal's power, produces a thinner bottom line.

With this first setting out of the way, the marina area then offers a capsule view of the lake environment.

"When you launch your boat, turn on your sonar and leave it on automatic. The object is to get over the deeper water of the marina and start turning in circles. Pay attention to what the screen is showing. You'll start seeing activity at a certain depth, and this depth (in summer, when lakes are stratified in thermal layers) will show the presence of a thermocline."

For anglers trying to locate bass in the summer season, accurately identifying the depth of this thermocline, or temperature breakline, is critical. In addition to serving as a temperature barrier that pushes gamefish to the water above, thermoclines often collect baitfish at this depth. Although thermoclines may be harder to discern at other times during the

Pro Profile
DON IOVINO
Hometown: Burbank, Calif.
Birthdate: 6-16-1938

BASS Career Highlights
Tournament Titles: Not yet won a Bassmaster title.
Times in the Classic: 0
Times in the Money: 6
Total Weight: 377 lbs., 7 ozs.
Career Winnings: $5,780
Avg. Per Tournament: $240.83

Don Iovino is a veteran Western angler whose deep water expertise spans three decades.

day, at first light, this temperature gradient is usually fairly obvious.

Appearing much like a gently undulating band of sketchy, thin lines (similar to a bottom gray line but less distinct), the thermocline serves as a good tool for quickly pinpointing the productive depth in summer. Quite simply, it tells a fisherman two important things: (1) Most of the catchable fish will be somewhere above this depth, and (2) structure located at this depth (a submerged island, hump or point) can offer the best fish catching opportunities.

In most summer situations, Iovino recommends placing the sensitivity setting at 70 percent, since enhanced plankton growth during the warmer months can lead to a cluttered picture at higher percentages. Then, it's simply a matter of placing the gray line value at 50 percent, switching to the automatic depth mode and starting to fish.

Precisely where to fish demands some homework, experience and perhaps a little intuition.

When fishing an unfamiliar lake, Iovino often reverts to a tried-and-true formula: Find the dam. In his experience, the creek channels and points around dam areas invariably offer the best odds in locating some fish.

When you begin fishing is when the sonar learning curve starts. By using sonar to select the key part of any structure — an area with a harder bottom, more pronounced depth change, presence of baitfish, isolated cover or other irregularities — a fisherman can spend more time working productive water.

After carefully marking the spot and making presentations from several different angles, Iovino generally spends no more than 15 minutes on a single area.

"There is a brief window when the fish are active. If you keep returning to the spots you've found with sonar, sooner or later one of those windows will open," offers Iovino.

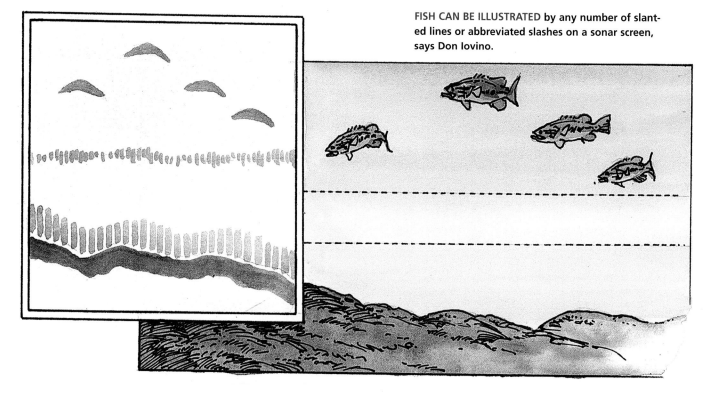

FISH CAN BE ILLUSTRATED by any number of slanted lines or abbreviated slashes on a sonar screen, says Don Iovino.

"If you're not getting bit, the next best thing to do is move to the bank near those same areas. Many times, bass will not eat a bait presented in a certain way. Throwing out from the bank and working a lure uphill sometimes gives a more natural look." In some cases, the bass may have moved to shallower water, in which case you also will want to throw to the bank.

In learning to interpret sonar, the most significant exercise is in comparing what is on the screen where you *don't* catch fish to what's there when you did. In the best case scenarios, the differences — depth, type of cover, structure, presence or position of baitfish, bottom composition, etc. — are obvious. In time, even subtle factors become readily apparent.

Even when apparently identical spots do not produce identical results, the experienced angler will know enough to look beyond the sonar screen to the position of these areas in relation to major lake features, wind direction, current, time of day or other "big picture" factors that make one area more productive than the next.

While the process of interpreting sonar information begins with understanding how to properly set up the sonar unit, it has no end point.

Every fishing situation, every day, presents a new angling puzzle to unravel. The ultimate payoff comes when things learned today produce bass a year or two from now.

THE MOST CHALLENGING TASK in reading sonar is learning to discern what is on the screen when you catch bass from what was present when you went fishless.

INDEX